ANGER MANAGEMENT

Advance Praise for *Anger Management*

'I am a physician and a strong believer in spiritual practices. I found this book to be an amazing dissertation on practical, thoughtful and spiritual solutions to a major problem I have seen in all my patients. This treatise is both scientifically sound and gives a very practical programme of action to address the well described problem of living with anger.'

—Daniel Fink, MD, occupational and environmental medicine physician

'One of the things that surprised me about this book was the detailed explanation of the neurological, psychological and biological aspects of anger at the very beginning. The author also discusses the external and internal triggers of anger, providing perfect examples that demonstrate how anger can shut off our intelligence. These examples range from daily situations to examples from Hindu philosophy, making it easy for readers of all ages to understand. What sets this book apart is its accessibility; it is written in a way that anyone can understand it, regardless of their cultural background or experience with psychology.'

—**Padmaja Puppala, MD, certified addiction psychiatrist**

'Perhaps now more than ever people seem to be expressing their anger with hostility and violence. Whether it is an incident of road rage or an exchange of unpleasant words with a disgruntled co-worker or spouse, we encounter outbursts of anger nearly every day.

'This manual helps readers identify common internal and external triggers in daily situations and discusses the negative aspects of anger on one's health. Readers will learn a practical approach for governing one's anger, including many from Hindu philosophy. These straightforward techniques are listed as clever acronyms, making them easy for readers to remember and implement. Regardless of one's religious background or knowledge on the subject, *Anger Management* is written in a manner that makes it accessible to all.'

—**Adria C. Savino, MD, addiction psychiatrist**

ANGER MANAGEMENT

A MONK'S WISDOM FOR
PERSONAL FULFILLMENT AND
PROFESSIONAL ACHIEVEMENT

Yugal Kishore Das

HARPER
VANTAGE

HarperCollins *Publishers* India

First published in India in 2023 by Harper Vantage
An imprint of HarperCollins *Publishers*
4th Floor, Tower A, Building No. 10, DLF Cyber City,
DLF Phase II, Gurugram, Haryana – 122002
www.harpercollins.co.in

2 4 6 8 10 9 7 5 3 1

P-ISBN: 978-93-5699-899-5
E-ISBN: 978-93-5699-398-3

Typeset in 12/15.7 Palatino Linotype at
Manipal Technologies Limited, Manipal

Printed and bound at
Thomson Press (India) Ltd

MIX
Paper from
responsible sources
FSC® C010615

FSC
www.fsc.org

This book is produced from independently certified FSC® paper
to ensure responsible forest management.

To my dear spiritual master,
H.H. Radhanath Swami

Contents

Foreword

The Art and Science of Self-Mastery by my dear friend, Yugal Kishore Das, presents practical insights into stress, anger and time management. By combining powerful stories with life lessons, illustrations to reflect and remember, and questions at the end of each chapter to help you on a sincere journey towards self-mastery, Das offers a pragmatic guide to enhance your professional and personal lives. Grounded in the foundations of Vedic wisdom, Das comes up with a handy manual that allows us to look into our inner mirror. Covered by the dust of our imperfections—anger, greed, envy and pride—we are unable to see our reflections clearly in that mirror. Das offers valuable tools to clean this mirror so we can see ourselves clearly.

In the summer of 2022, I was approached by Dr Ramana Vinjamuri, our common friend and well-wisher, to write the foreword for this important contribution. Vinjamuri described the significance and the practical wisdom offered in these books for each and everyone of us. Inspired by our conversation, I quickly took to reading the manuscripts and could not put them down. Having been thus exhilarated, I found immense pleasure in writing this foreword.

I have known Yugal Kishore Das for more than twenty years. When I first met him, he was working as a software consultant with MetLife insurance company in Albany, New York. He would help arrange programmes for me in Albany. I would stay at his house during weekends. This programme eventually shaped into a university programme where we were preaching to the students at State University of New York, Albany. Many students were benefitted from this programme. This engagement made us good friends. He eventually received initiation from my spiritual master and became my spiritual brother and this brought us closer. He would regularly come to our monastery in Manhattan to understand the life of a monk. In that association, he felt that human life is meant for self-realization and this can be attained by selflessly serving humanity. This eventually led him to give up his job and join a monastery in West Virginia. I really appreciated his courage and sacrifice. He sacrificed his job and life for the benefit of others. Time and distance have not proved to be obstacles in our brotherhood. We regularly preached together on several occasions. He started extensively travelling and preaching the message all over America. It is for the benefit of the people that he writes these books.

There was once a retreat in Palace of Gold in West Virginia which I attended with other monks in our monastery. There was a discussion on the causes of various problems of the world. I remember Yugal Kishore Das saying that envy, anger and greed are the problems of mankind and by practising spirituality sincerely, one can eventually become free from these unwanted impurities of the heart. External problems are the outcome of internal problems. It was a lively discussion and other monks also shared their perspectives on the problems of the world. Why are oceans and rivers polluted? It is because every heart is polluted. Since the population is very large, this inner pollution would naturally reflect in rivers and oceans in a big way. So, ecological problems have a connection with the lack of spirituality in society and real spirituality must focus on cleansing the heart with an aim to leading a pure life. That way the world will become a better place to live in for everyone.

We met many times in this way and shared and expressed our opinions. Whenever we met, we would sit together and meditate for hours in the mornings. This has helped develop a camaraderie between us. I strongly feel this book will be beneficial to many as he has shared his valuable realizations and experiences.

There are three books in this series: *Stress Management, Anger Management* and *Time Management*. Each of these books is self-contained and written in an easy-to-understand manner with practical and eye-opening lessons embedded in each chapter. Each chapter ends with few questions that make you think and explore your inner self. The author has penned these parts and chapters in such a way that the reader can turn to any page and find something meaningful and pragmatic. By encouraging you to remember and recollect what you have read in the text, the illustrations help guide you further.

In *Time Management,* Yugal Kishore Das, emphasizing the importance of how time is precious, shares key principles of time management and why we need to manage our time, as well as the kind of obstacles that hinder us when we put these principles to practice. This is where we realize why we are unable to implement these familiar yet fruitful practices into our routines. The simplicity and clarity with which these tips are described will encourage each one of us to implement them in our daily lives and benefit from the author's wisdom.

In *Anger Management*, the author starts by describing the nuts and bolts of anger. The readers will be pleasantly surprised with insightful lessons where the author reveals how our anger shuts off our intelligence and acts against us. When we reach the peak of heightened anger in the spur of a moment, what we never think of are the consequences of our actions taken during those weak moments. If we are aware of these consequences, we would at least think before taking any action. The author takes a holistic approach on how we can prevent anger by understanding our inner self, our lifestyle and our thought process. Das closes this part with some sensible techniques on anger management. By presenting simple formulas and equations, he reveals our inner psyche. For example, the author talks about 7–38–55 rule in effective communication where it is not simply about our words. Only 7 per cent is the choice of words, 38 per cent is tone of voice and a majority, 55 per cent is our body language. Our body language and tone depend on our mood and mentality. The author guides us on nourishing and nurturing our inner self to groom our mood and mentality.

In *Stress Management*, Das begins with a touching story of his interaction with a student. Just with this one incident, I am confident that the readers can relate to and understand that stress is part of everyone's dictionary. He explains the fundamentals of stress and different stressors—knowledge derived from Vedic wisdom. He further talks about the lifecycle of stress. Awareness about these topics somehow brings a sense of calmness within us. Perhaps because we are able to understand that we are not the only ones stressed out and it gives out the hope that even if we are in the dark now, there will be light sooner than later. In the next chapters, Das gets into the details of the internal and external factors of stress and how these affect our body and mind. At this point, instead of stressing on stress, he takes us on an uplifting and optimistic journey on how we can avoid stress, and suggests some preventive measures using the principles of effective communication and anxiety management. Finally, he closes by presenting a practical skill set on how to manage stress. These are some of my favourite parts of the book as they present methods on how to practise forgiveness, gratitude and service. The readers are left at this point with key practices on relaxation, meditation and prayer.

In summary, I am confident that you will learn meaningful lessons in every page of this book just as I did. I encourage you to use these lessons, respond to the questions he poses at the end of each chapter, remember the tips and reflect on them, and, finally, adapt and apply them in your personal and professional lives.

As a techie, as a software engineer working for multinational companies, as a counsellor, as a life coach and as a monk in the West, Yugal Kishore Das had trekked a unique journey. From this unique journey comes his unique insights into the inner engineering that enables each one of us to turn our weaknesses such as anger, stress, sense of inferiority and procrastination into our strengths such as inner peace, composure, determination and confidence.

Pandit Dasa
mindful leadership expert and
motivational speaker,
USA Today's 'Top 8 Influential Speakers to
Follow' in 2002,
author of bestsellers *Urban Monk* and
Closing the Apps
For more information, please
visit: www.panditdasa.com

Preface

Usually, it is medical doctors and research scientists who write books on such topics. So, what made me (a monk) write these books?

As technology started developing with a singular motive to make our lives better, paradoxically and interestingly, our lives started becoming more and more mechanical. Despite technology being at its peak today, we all have become very disoriented in our lives. In the US alone, an astounding number of people have mental health problems. We live in the time of a lot of social unrest.

Why is there so much social unrest globally? It is because everyone is experiencing a lot of internal unrest, one within themselves. Why is there this unrest at an individual and internal level? When we face disturbance on a physical, mental or emotional level, it disturbs or inner peace. Apart from this, nature too offers us challenges in the form of extreme weather, cyclones, floods, earthquakes and tsunamis, etc. In this world where everyone is quarrelling with each other, there is always somebody or something that seems to disturb our peace. Mental and physical ailments also cause us a lot of stress. Apart from this, the world of today is becoming increasingly global. Hence, a slight disturbance caused in one part of the world spirals out to affect people in the other part of the world, making them frustrated and depressed. Stress, anxiety, frustration and depression have become the buzz words in this busy world.

Managing our stress, anger and time on a daily basis has become especially difficult. Everyone seems to be extremely busy. But by the end of the hectic day, they realize that they have truly accomplished only a little. This makes them unhappy.

Stress is a common problem in society. We all have a list of things to address. Some demand our immediate attention. But we may not have enough resources to manage these tasks or to deal with the resultant stress.

When we are busy addressing and sorting out everyday problems all the time, our body finds itself constantly in the fight-and-flight mode, with very little rest. In such a state, things are bound to go wrong, and, as a result, we also become angry.

How do we make ourselves immune to all these problems? That is the subject matter of these books. For example, we must understand that we have no control over tomorrow's weather or how our boss is going to act with us, but we have control over how *we* react. By developing the right mindset and/or by taking precautionary measures, we can either minimize the problem or totally avoid the problem. For example, if the tree is healthy and strong and firmly rooted deep within the soil, it can weather any type of storms or overcome threats posed by any type of pests. In the same way, if we can become strong and firm, we can face the storms of life. What are the tools we need to make us firmly rooted within ourselves to face any type of disturbance or adversity in our lives?

I write these books to equip people with the necessary tools needed to deal with the common problems of life that we all face on a day-to-day basis. First step in that direction is awareness and acceptance of the problems, and recognizing the need to address them. Of course, for that to happen, we need to have a very good understanding of our mind and sense organs, and their collective functioning in both relaxed as well as problematic environments.

Since the mind, as opposed to the brain, is not a physical organ but a very intangible one, its behaviour is unpredictable and differs from individual to individual. Once, I was conducting a seminar in a college on the positive attitude of the mind. After the seminar, a student came to me and said, 'If only you had come two weeks ago and conducted this seminar, my friend would not have committed suicide.' Moved, I asked him why he felt like that. He said, the presentation was mentally very uplifting and gave so much hope and strength to deal with the problems of life.

During my research, I was fascinated to find how our mind operates differently at different times and different environments. It is very interesting to note that our mind picks up all of the information that we gullibly and inadvertently collect through our various experiences. But when we want to erase it from our mind, it is not easy to erase them. These thoughts circulate in our minds for a very long time. I tried to find the relation between the nature around us, our impulsive thoughts and the reactions of the body to them. The reality is our senses constantly demand enjoyment. But our mind being connected to our senses has the ability control them. However, the mind is fickle and gets distracted easily, without bothering about the consequences. This is a serious problem, and many people are not aware of this problem. Intelligence is superior to the mind and hence can control the senses. If we can sharpen our intelligence and control the mind, our life becomes much better. In fact, learning this truth led me to take up the meditation process more seriously, whereby I tried to restrain the demands of the mind and the senses with a sharpened intelligence.

I have been meditating for more than twenty-five years on a daily basis. I am myself fascinated with the results. I was part of Henry Ford Hospital research team which conducted research on the efficacy of mantra meditation (where you meditate by chanting on a mantra) and its effect on the brain. Based on my experience in dealing with the mind, I have developed a few tools and a lifestyle whereby one can handle anxiety and stress. With these tools, I have been counselling hundreds of professionals from the corporate world, as well as many families and students for more than twenty-one years in the US and other countries, and have helped them cope with stress, anxiety, anger and depression.

My training is based on imparting knowledge on the internal aspects of our physical bodies—their functioning and their inter-relationships.

I provide separate tools to handle the physical body, the internal space of the mind and the deeper intellect. When we realize that we, as consciousness, are different from our physical organs and that it is our thoughts that lead us to action, we become careful with our thought process. This is where we need help and training. With proper guidance and practice, we can alter various negative patterns of our mind to positive patterns, and bring a revolutionary change in our actions and in our lives.

I have mentioned many examples and case studies in these books for the benefit of the reader. If you are able to get some benefit out of them, I will be most happy as a monk and consider this little endeavour fruitful.

Your humble servant,
Yugal Kishore Das
Michigan (USA), 17 July 2023

CHAPTER 1

The Nuts and Bolts of Anger

1.1. EMOTIONAL REACTION OR RATIONAL RESPONSE?

Anger is a widespread disease. Though a completely normal emotion, when left uncontrolled, anger can cause some serious problems. It's not all bad though. One manifestation of anger is its appearing as a built-in response to danger; for this purpose, it can sometimes be useful. More often than not, however, anger appears as an emotional reaction to something we don't like. If unchecked, this kind of anger damages our health and ruins our relationships. In this section, we'll primarily deal with how to manage and ultimately eliminate this kind of anger.

The Oxford dictionary defines anger as a strong feeling of annoyance, displeasure or hostility. When things go against our desires, we often feel these emotions pop up. When we're stuck in a traffic jam while trying to get to the office and someone cuts us off, we may start to feel some hostility bubbling. When our children neglect their chores, we may naturally feel some annoyance. When our least favourite person at the office nabs the last slice of pizza at the office party, some displeasure may start to swell.

To tell the difference between good anger and bad anger, we should consider the ultimate results that it produces. If a mother sometimes uses anger in a controlled way to instil proper values and a strong work ethic in her children, then her use of the emotion is beneficial. If you speed up in an attempt to return the favour when someone cuts you off on the road and you end up accidentally crashing into the person in front of you, that anger is detrimental. We may conclude that the quality of anger depends on the level of control with which it's used and the intent behind using it. When used in a controlled manner for a good cause, anger is a rational response, but when we ourselves are used by anger and forced to act with malicious intent, it is a dangerous emotional reaction.

1.2. ANGER IS ONE LETTER SHORT OF DANGER

Anger leads to suffering and unlimited loss.

—Buddha

When we are agitated by anger, we tend to speak harshly and sometimes use abusive language. Subjecting someone to angry words is like hammering nails into their heart. Apologizing may remove the nails, but the damage will have already been done. It often takes a long time for the holes to heal, and even after they do, the scars remain.

Besides the effect it can have on others, anger also greatly contributes to cardiovascular diseases and diabetes. In the heat of the moment, people tend to say and do things that their natural, rational self would be appalled by. This is the exact plight of many souls who now sit in prison cells, regretting the actions they once resorted to in the heat of the moment. Other people deal with their anger by taking intoxicants, a sure-fire path to addiction. These choices result from the workings of minds that are vastly handicapped by an overwhelming emotion. In such a state, one's intelligence and powers of discernment are greatly impaired.

DANGER

In 2001, the news of the assassination of Nepal's King Birendra shocked the world. One night, when the royal family assembled at the dinner table, the king's son, Prince Dipendra, brought up his desire to marry his girlfriend. The royal family rejected the idea completely. Overwhelmed with rage, the prince retrieved an assault rifle and shot his father, mother, other family members and himself dead on the spot. This is, of course, an extreme example, but it illustrates the extent to which discernment can be impaired when anger goes unchecked.

Think about the last time you got angry and consider the questions below.

- Did you express your anger appropriately the last time you got angry?
- Was getting angry the most effective approach to the situation?
- Was the intensity of anger expressed proportionate to the situation?

1.3. ANGER SHUTS OFF OUR INTELLIGENCE

When we keep our cool, we're able to use our intelligence to weigh different options before making a decision. In this state, we're free to deeply analyse a given problem from different angles and consider the immediate and long-term consequences of choosing one response over another. When we become angry, however, this discerning ability is thrown out the window. Anger causes us to act immediately, without considering anything except how to avenge our displeasure.

To understand this concept, we need to understand how our brain functions on anger. Of particular importance in this regard are two areas of the brain: the prefrontal cortex and the amygdala. The amygdala, consisting of two almond-shaped structures located deep within the portion of the brain known as the temporal lobe, is a part of the brain's limbic system, which is involved in emotional and behavioural responses, particularly those behaviours needed for survival. It is responsible for handling flight or fight situations. It identifies relationships between emotions and events and stores those relationships for future reference. When it senses danger, it immediately reacts and starts releasing hormones to prepare us to either fight or run away to safety. The prefrontal cortex, which is part of the frontal lobe of the brain, is responsible for planning, executive functioning, reasoning, impulse control, emotional regulation, considering consequences and intelligent decision-making.

When a situation causes anger or stress, the amygdala reacts to the situation and prepares us for fight or flight without giving the frontal lobe an opportunity to react—it reacts without receiving any signal from us for action. This instantaneous, overwhelming reaction—termed 'amygdala hijack'—can often be an overreaction, and this explains why, when we are angry, it often seems like our intelligence shuts down and our responses become very quick. In fact, the key solution to anger lies here. If we can make the prefrontal cortex react to the situation instead of the amygdala, we will react coolly instead of bursting with anger. How to do that is explained in the upcoming chapters.

The following story provides another example of swift action without consideration of consequences as a result of unbridled anger.

There was once a couple that yearned for a child. When they were blessed with a baby boy, their love for him knew no bounds. The family of three had a loyal pet mongoose that guarded their home from dangerous creatures. One day, while the father was away at work and the mother was busy in the backyard, the mongoose saw a snake making its way to the cradle in which the baby was asleep. To protect the baby, the mongoose attacked the snake and tore it to pieces. When the father returned and saw the mongoose at the doorstep with blood dripping from its mouth, he falsely assumed that the mongoose had killed his baby, and in a fit of anger, he beat the mongoose to death with his stick. He then ran inside to assess the situation and saw that his baby was safe in his cradle, beneath which lay the remains of the snake. Realizing that the mongoose had saved his baby, the father was overcome with guilt.

Anger does not call us and make an appointment to meet us at a certain time. It comes like a force of nature, at the least expected moment. Before we realize it, we are taken over by anger, and we end up fully involving ourselves in verbal exchanges or sometimes physical fights that only waste our time and undermine our happiness.

When children are exposed to the angry outbursts and regular quarrels of their parents, they develop fear and insecurity. Their mental growth is also stunted. They never forget the intense incidents of their childhood. They are tormented by the memories. For the sake of their children, parents should not quarrel before them.

When you understand the repercussions of anger, you will hopefully restrain yourself from becoming angry.

1.4. ANGER AS AN ACID

> *Anger is an acid that can do more harm to the vessel in which it is stored than to the thing on which it is thrown.*
>
> —Mark Twain

Anger burns and hurts those attacked by it. But, by harbouring it within us, we do much more damage to ourselves. This fact manifests on both gross and subtle levels. A couple of diseases we can incur by harbouring anger have already been mentioned, but the ailments don't end there. We're also liable to suffer muscle tension, headaches, digestive disorders and various forms of mental illness because of anger.

Anger burns us first

One day, Tom, a teenager, went to a nearby lake, sat on his boat and started to meditate with his eyes closed. He soon internalized his consciousness, gained control of his mind and began to relish a deep sense of calm within. Suddenly, his boat was hit by another boat, causing a sudden jerk. Tom—his trance broken by a sense of intense fear—felt an adrenaline rush followed by the swelling of intense anger—'Is this person blind or what? Can't he see me here?' Without opening his eyes, he then tried to subdue his ill feelings and regain the peace he had previously attained.

A few minutes later, his boat was hit again! This time, his anger skyrocketed. His eyes turned red as he grimaced with rage—'What's wrong with this guy?! Does he think I'm weak and can't teach him a lesson?' His mind reeled with a burning desire to avenge the egregious insult. Finally giving in, he opened his eyes, ready to start throwing every cuss word he could think of at the jerk before him. Then he realized the boat that was bumping into him was empty and had been pushed into his boat by the wind. Finally able to take a step back, he was struck by how far his anger had taken him from his desired peace. He realized that his enemy was not some phantom boatman but the force of anger itself.

1.5. ANGER TRIGGERS

In order to combat anger, it's important to consider the triggers that provoke it. These can generally be broken down into two categories: internal and external. Let us take a deeper look at these triggers so as to better understand how to deal with them.

External Triggers

There are unlimited opportunities to get angry on a daily basis. Perhaps your spouse sleepily switched off your alarm in the morning and you woke up late for work. Then, you went to the bathroom and saw that your kids had once again misplaced the toothpaste. Then, you rushed out to the car only to realize that your teenager had left it on an empty tank the night before. Can you feel the fire? There are, of course, some triggers we all tend to experience. See if you can relate to any of these:

- Being made fun of
- Being disrespected

- Being physically threatened
- Having your trust betrayed
- Dealing with chronic pain
- Failing to get enough sleep

We may notice that a common thread running through all the above is the obstruction of the desire to enjoy pleasure and avoid discomfort. Can you think of any other examples of external forces that may obstruct this desire?

Internal Triggers

Now let us consider some of the less obvious but often more powerful triggers—those originating within us. For many people, at different times in their lives, anger can start to feel like a state of being. This kind of subtle, ever-present anger is perhaps the most detrimental, as it affects each and every thing we do and say in our day-to-day lives. Do you recognize any of these internal triggers affecting your life?

- Unfulfilled desires
- Egoism
- Frustration
- Envy
- The desire to control others

While external triggers are largely unavoidable, those perceived within can be curbed. Practicing self-restraint when there is an internal trigger will help largely improve the landscape of our lives. Let us take a deeper look at each of these culprits so as to be able to spot them when they appear within our hearts.

Unfulfilled Desires

Intrinsically, each and every one of us carries a desire for unmitigated happiness. As a result, we have unmitigated desires for different kinds of enjoyment—food, money, luxury, sex, etc. This manifests in the form of a constant search for the next hit of pleasure. The mind thus tends to obsess over different kinds of potential enjoyment we may experience. The ancient wisdom texts declare that when we meditate upon desired objects we become attached to them, and from this attachment comes an intense desire to acquire them; as a result of this unfulfilled desire, anger arises. Consider the following illustration of this phenomenon at work.

On your way to your place of work, you're likely to see upwards of a hundred products being advertised to you daily—a new car, a new fast-food creation, a new piece of jewellery, etc. The reason

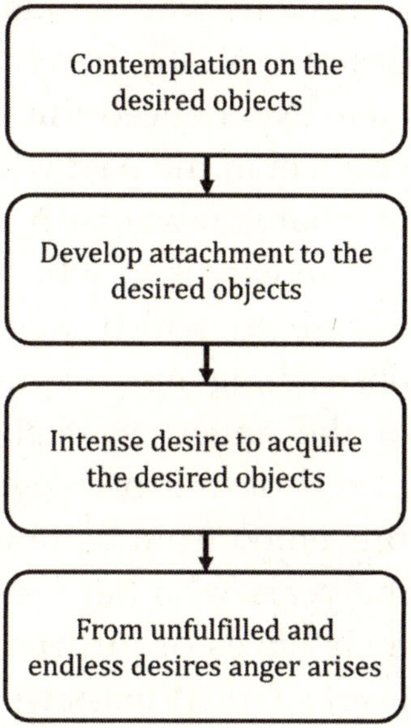

billboard advertising is a multi-million-dollar industry is simple: the more people see something, the more likely they are to desire it. The thought of buying a new car may pass through your mind almost unnoticed, but if you see an ad for the kind of car you were thinking of, the thought might then take root. If you then begin researching the car, the thought can turn into a strong desire. Having taken root in your mind, the desire then blossoms into a huge purchase that likely wasn't required in the first place. In this cycle of thinking, feeling and willing, thoughts turn into intense cravings and eventually manifest as purchases.

Now let's say this intense desire for a new car is shot down by your spouse, who instead desires to use a chunk of that disposable income to go visit some friends on the other side of the country. Because your desire has been rejected, your anger is likely to rise and a heated argument is likely to ensue.

Anyone who stands in the way of our object of desire typically becomes Enemy #1. Perhaps you have experienced this dynamic. How did it make you feel in the past when someone got in the way of what you wanted?

The extent to which we crave an object is the degree to which we become angry with those obstructing our acquisition of it. That intensity of the anger we feel comes from the intensity of our desire to enjoy whatever it is we're being prevented from having. Think of all the men over the years who have killed each other for stealing their wives or girlfriends—such depravities have even sparked massive wars. Never underestimate the potential consequences of anger born of an obstructed desire. Can you think of any times in your life when you've witnessed someone become enraged by a blocked craving?

Here's another example.

You and your family are visiting your friend along with a few other people. As your friend shows you around his home, you become fascinated by the facilities. You see the others complimenting him for having acquired such a wonderful place. As a result, you develop a desire for a similar home. You go through the thinking, feeling and willing stages, and the desire becomes stronger and stronger. Initially, the desire is feeble, like a piece of cotton that you can crush and throw in the trash. But when desire crosses the stages of thinking, feeling and willing, it becomes strong and hard, like a stone. When your spouse refuses to concede to your desire to buy a new home, you become angry at them as you feel they are obstructing your enjoyment.

There is a wonderful story in the ancient Indian scriptures that also depicts the above mentality.

Sunda and Upasunda were both brothers from a demon race. They were very fond of harassing people. They wanted to become immortal; hence, they both performed intense austerities to gain the favour of the Creator. When the Creator, Brahma, appeared, they both prayed that they would not be killed by anyone, but would die only when they killed each other. They were both brothers and good friends—they were very sure that there would never be any enmity between them and that they would thus live eternally without any problems. When Brahma granted them this wish, they felt they had conquered death.

They became very powerful and started conquering the heavenly planets and harassing everyone, including even the powerful celestial beings. The celestials complained to Brahma, saying that as a result of his munificence, Sunda and Upasunda had become invincible. They had no idea what to do to end the brothers' menacing reign.

Brahma pacified the celestials and devised a plan. He created a beautiful celestial damsel named Tilottama and instructed her to work according to his plan. As per Brahma's instructions, Tilottama met the demon brothers separately. They were both enamoured by her beauty, and both of them developed the intense desire to marry her.

When the brothers met and shared the news of their imminent marriage with each other, they realized they were trying to marry the same person. Neither wanted to give up his aspiration for the sake of the other. Both felt the other was unjustly obstructing their enjoyment. This made them so furious at each other that they became enemies. In their anger, they picked up their clubs and fought to the death.

The moral of the story: when someone obstructs or tries to obstruct our happiness, we become angry with them.

Egoism

Each of us has an ego that comes with the desire to be in control all the time. Disregarding what the laws of karma may justly dictate, everyone tends to view himself or herself as the supreme enjoyer, the person whose enjoyment everything and everyone else is meant for. If someone agrees with us, we consider them a friend; if someone disagrees with us, they become our enemy. When things go our way, we feel we've made them happen by the power of our will alone. When things go against our wishes, we blame others. In contrast to this mentality, the ancient wisdom texts declare that five key factors contribute to all actions:

1. Desire
2. The physical body
3. The senses
4. The endeavour itself
5. Divine sanction

The first four are quite self-explanatory; it is the last one that we often tend to forget. What is the difference between two people who work equally hard for the same goal, with the same degree of intelligence and dedication, but ultimately achieve very different results? The sanction of the ultimate authority, without which not even a blade of grass moves. A spiritualist understands this principle deeply and thus cultivates humility. Understanding that we are ultimately not in control keeps the disease of egoism far away. Avoiding this illusion of control allows us to better control our temper when things don't go as planned.

Ravana was the King of Lanka (present-day Sri Lanka, in Southeast Asia), an achiever who performed many austerities and acquired many supernatural powers as a result, enabling him to defeat all his opponents. But lust was his Achilles heel.

Sita was the supremely beautiful goddess of fortune and the wife of Rama, the incarnation of God. When Ravana heard about Sita, he became infatuated and abducted her. Many elders tried to convince Ravana to undo this thoughtless act, but he paid no attention to them. His brother Vibhishan used many different strategies to try and reform him, providing Ravana with all kinds of logical reasons to consider changing his ways. Ravana saw his brother as a threat to his enjoyment; he did not heed his advice. At one point, he became so angry with Vibhishan that he drove him away from his kingdom. He was so confident of his strength that he thought he could do whatever he wanted. However, eventually he was killed by Rama in battle. This is an example of egoistic behaviour.

Resentment

When our basic needs are not respected in our relationships with others, naturally some resentment towards them starts to brew. This lapse in respect is often witnessed in the form of a superior in the workplace exploiting us. The employees may tolerate the offensive behaviour for some time, but if their feelings remain untended, they may eventually explode in anger. This phenomenon is also witnessed in children who suffer from neglect at home. Children who aren't properly cared for tend to develop a strong resentment against their parents that often explodes in the form of rebellion once they hit their teens.

Consider the following story about the ill effects of a resentful attitude.

Drupada and Drona were not only classmates but close friends. Drupada was the son of the king, whereas Drona hailed from a poor family. Drupada would often mention to Drona that he would help him in the future when needed. After they graduated from school, life took them on different routes. Drupada succeeded his father and became the king. Drona, unable to find a suitable job, led a life of poverty.

One day, when Drona's son asked him for milk, he felt very bad that he could not afford any. At this time, he remembered Drupada's promise. He went to Drupada's court and sought help. Instead of helping him, Drupada ridiculed him and said, 'Friendship is between equals. I am a king, and you are a poor and unworthy soul. Don't remind me of our past friendship. I will help you if you come to me as a beggar.' He then offered Drona a little charity.

When Drona heard these insulting words, he became exceedingly angry; his heart longed for revenge. He later acquired celestial weapons from warrior Parasuram. By the will of providence, he became the martial arts teacher of five pandava princes and one-hundred kaurava princes. He taught them archery and other fighting skills. He shared with them the knowledge of using celestial weapons on the battlefield. At the end of their training, when his students asked him about the favour he wanted from them as his students, he asked for Drupada as a slave.

All Kuarva princes tried capturing Drupada in battle but failed. Later Pandava princes engaged Drupada in war and made him their prisoner. He eventually had his disciples defeat Drupada.

When Drupada was captured and brought before him as a prisoner, Drona said, 'You are my slave now and your kingdom is mine. But I remember our past friendship, so I will let you go and rule the kingdom.' Drupada felt humiliated and became angry, and his heart longed for revenge. They thus remained lifelong enemies.

We all experience situations that provoke resentment within us from time to time, but it is important to make sure we're not letting those negative emotions build up. It is better to seek counsel from a close friend, relative or even a therapist than to internalize our frustration. You'd be surprised at how powerful the simple act of sharing one's feelings can be. This can be compared to gradually releasing air from a balloon instead of popping it. When you feel like you are under too much pressure or you are too full of a certain emotion, find someone you can trust to help you relieve it.

Frustration

When our basic needs are not fulfilled or when someone exploits us because of our weak status or position, we get frustrated. And if the situation persists, it triggers our anger.

If a manager exploits his employee, the employee will tolerate it for some time. But the anger builds up due to frustration, until one day it erupts like a volcano. Anger at the workplace is common. Being mocked or bullied by someone in a higher position is frustrating, but we are obliged to tolerate it. When the situation eventually becomes intolerable, we explode.

Let us analyse the anger of children due to frustration. When children don't get the love and support they need from their homes, they feel insecure. When their basic needs—like food, proper sleep and help with homework— are not met, their frustration builds. When their problems continue to mount but there is no support system that can be drawn on to solve them, their frustration eventually turns into wrath and manifests in very unhealthy ways. This is how resentment forms.

Long ago, there was a family with a prodigal son by the name of Bharavi. Even as a child, he was very scholarly and widely acclaimed for his compositions in the ancient Sanskrit language. But his talent was not recognized by his father, who never appreciated him, remained indifferent to his poetic talents and even belittled his son's achievements. As Bharavi grew up, his poetic talents and fame grew as well and so did his father's indifference towards his achievements. This triggered a lot of resentment in the heart of Bharavi, as his patient wait for his father's approval proved futile year after year.

Eventually, his resentment turned into uncontrollable rage. He decided to kill his father. One day, when his parents were talking, he secretly overheard their conversation. His mother asked his father why he did not recognize his son's poetic talents and achievements. His father said that he knew of his son's poetic talents and no one was happier about his son's success. But, at the same time, he feared that Bharavi would become proud, which would ruin everything. Hence, he was visibly indifferent to Bharavi's achievements, even though they made him feel happiness within. Having heard all this, Bharavi came to his senses, fell at the feet of his father and asked for forgiveness.

Although the father had the best interests of his son at heart, in hindsight, completely depriving him of appreciation may not have been the correct approach. Providing even a little appreciation could have prevented the resentment from growing.

We need to make sure our frustration does not mount. If it does, then we need to share our problem(s) with someone we trust. If it remains a problem, we should take help from counsellors, psychiatrists or other sources of support that we will explore in the chapters ahead.

Envy

Envy is an interesting trigger for anger. One can observe its influence on oneself or on others on a regular basis. Because material desires can never be truly satisfied—only replaced with more material desires—we tend to develop a sense of competition with others; we want our desires be fulfilled in bigger and better ways than theirs are. When we see that someone we know is getting what we wanted or having their desires fulfilled in a grander way than we are fulfilling our desires, we become envious. From this envy comes a subtle but deep-seated anger that makes us constantly look for their faults in an effort to re-establish ourselves in a superior position. This anger is likely to boil over, causing us to lash out at the person whom we envy, thus further complicating our relationship with them and perpetuating feelings of ill-will.

This may remind some of the classic story of Cain and Abel from the biblical Book of Genesis. The two sons of Adam and Eve grew up together as loving brothers. Cain eventually became a farmer while Abel became a shepherd. One day, they both decided to make offerings to God. God praised Abel's offering as superior to Cain's. Burning with envy, Cain took his brother out into a field and killed him, an act that led to him later being condemned to wander for the rest of his life. Cain's disproportionate response shows us the effect that envy can have on the human psyche. Instead of allowing ourselves to be overcome with such pointless jealousy, we can acquire the proper foresight to deal with such situations. This will be discussed in the sections to come.

Desire to Control Others

Impelled by the ego and false prestige, as we mentioned earlier, we may consciously or subconsciously maintain a strong desire to control others. Under the guise of a desire for perfection, we try to control our dependents, significant others, friends and/or colleagues. The tendency is often so subtle that we don't even realize that we are being selfish and domineering; instead, we tend to admonish others for their shortcomings if they don't fall in line with our desires.

This tendency especially manifests when someone who was obedient to us in the past starts making their own independent decisions. We simply cannot tolerate the thought of someone slipping away from our web of influence. To cope and to justify our desire for control, we try to find fault with them. Instead of succumbing to this tendency to control others, we should understand that every individual is unique, with unique experiences and ways of looking at things. Recognizing this allows us to accept others and their decisions without feeling the need to impose ourselves and our decisions on them.

Summary

- Anger is a strong feeling of annoyance, displeasure or hostility.
- Anger shuts off our intelligence.
- Anger is one letter short of danger.

External Triggers

- Being made fun of
- Being disrespected
- Being physically threatened
- Having your trust betrayed
- Dealing with a physical ailment
- Failing to get enough sleep
- Something or someone blocking your enjoyment

Internal Triggers

- Unfulfilled desires
- Egoism
- Frustration
- Envy
- Desire to control others

Questions

1. Approximately how many times have you got angry in the past week?

____

____

____

____

2. What are your typical external triggers?

____

____

____

____

3. What are your internal triggers?

___

___

___

___

4. What personal experiences do you have of anger being close to danger?

___

___

___

___

CHAPTER 2

The Consequences of Anger

Anybody can become angry—that is easy, but to be angry with the right person, and to the right degree, and at the right time, and for the right purpose, and in the right way, that is not within everyone's power, that is not so easy.

—Aristotle

2.1. POSITIVE ASPECTS OF ANGER

Heightened Focus

As previously mentioned, our body reacts to anger in a very interesting way. Upon registering the anger-inducing stimulus, the brain immediately begins pumping catecholamines into our body, triggering a kind of super-focus and readiness. If we were to witness a

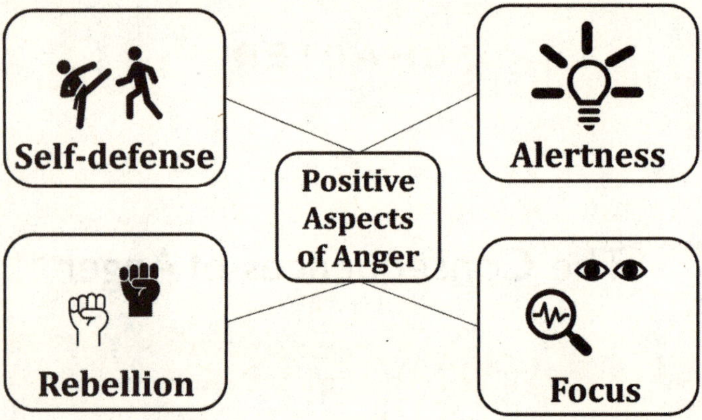

crazy person attack our family member, the anger and resultant awareness we'd experience would help us put an end to the situation. In this sense, anger can sometimes be used to protect those around us.

Heightened Alertness

Anger triggers adrenaline, and resultantly, our alertness in a given situation. I have seen many people who are normally soft-spoken and passive become almost electrified when informed of their wrongs. Being learned in the art of positive anger, they channel that energy into the job at hand, utilizing their newfound hyper-awareness to seek out and correct any and all imperfections with clarity and vigour.

Self-Defence

Sometimes people take the kindness and leniency of others for granted and start exploiting them. In such cases, a controlled exhibition of anger can be utilized to make things right. For example, we can call upon our old friend Hanuman, whom we've previously discussed.

While in Sri Lanka looking for King Ram's abducted wife Sita, Hanuman took on a tiny form so as to not be noticed. During his search, he was stopped by the demoness Lankini, who began chiding him for his embarrassingly small stature.

Lankini said, 'Hey monkey, stop! Who are you? Why have you come here?'

Hanuman replied, 'I'd heard of the beauty of Lanka and decided to come and see it for myself.'

Lankini guffawed. 'But this is our island! People like you are not allowed. I could kill you with a single slap.'

Hanuman humbly pleaded, 'I will stay here only for a short time. I only wish to see a few places. Then I will go back home. Please give me permission for a short visit.'

'Oh fool, tiny monkey, you want to see Lanka?! How dare you come here!' Lankini struck Hanuman hard, attempting to kill him. Hanuman survived the attack and became very angry with her for unjustly attacking him. After fighting for some time, he managed to ward her off and save his own life. In this way, Hanuman used the anger caused by her senseless attack to preserve his life, and ultimately, save the queen.

Rebelling against Injustice

Anger channelled into strategic planning and execution can yield seriously impactful results. When we become aware of someone's maltreatment of us or those close to us, the anger we resultantly feel can often be used to rectify the situation. So long as we approach the dilemma with a level head and channel our anger into proper planning and consideration, it may propel us towards positive change. A great historical example of this kind of positive anger was the Boston Tea Party protest of 1773. Angered by unjust taxation without their having any say in the matter, the American colonists made their feelings known by dumping 342 chests of British-imported tea into the Boston Harbour. This act of defiance helped inspire the entire nation to take up arms and fight for their liberty in the American Revolution. Mahatma Gandhi and Nelson Mandela also channelled the anger of their people into successful revolutions, kicking out their unjust oppressors for the sake of justice and freedom.

Gandhi led a non-violent Indian revolution to fight the injustice being meted out to Indians. He channelled the anger of all his followers in a constructive way to bring freedom to India. Following in his footsteps, Nelson Mandela led a peaceful revolution to bring freedom to South Africa.

In the Ramayana, Hanuman courageously went to the demon king Ravana as a messenger and warned him of the consequences of his abduction of Sita. He helped Lord Rama kill Ravana and rescue Sita.

2.2. NEGATIVE ASPECTS OF ANGER

Switches Off Discernment

When we become angry, our amygdala jumps into action without our authorization. It takes over the frontal lobe of the cortex, which is responsible for thinking and discerning. It immediately releases chemicals necessary for action. That is why anger switches off the power to discern. In a fit of anger, we may become so emotional that we blurt out invectives at others unintentionally. We act without thinking of the consequences.

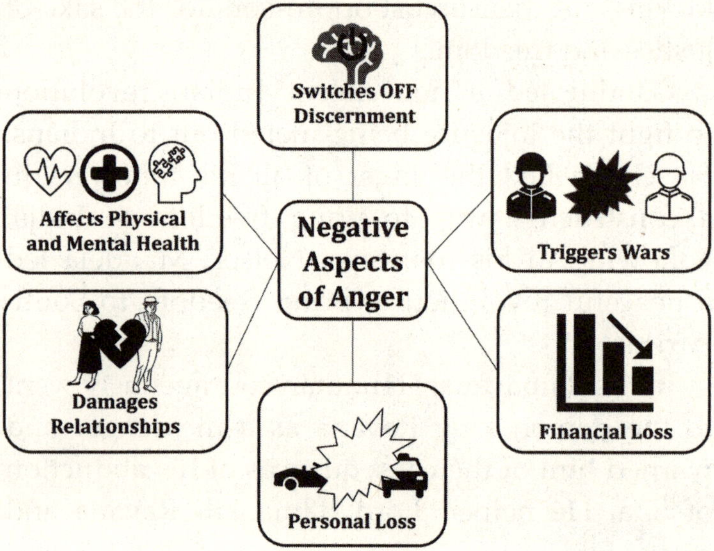

Affects Physical and Mental Health

To prepare the body to experience anger, the adrenal glands release two hormones, cortisol and adrenaline, which fill the body with energy. There is an increase in our heart rate and blood pressure. Blood is withdrawn from different parts of our body and sent to the muscles to energize them. In other words, the body works hard to effectively react to the perceived stimulus during the phase of anger. It takes a very long time for the body to return to its normal state.

When people experience angry outbursts regularly, they tend to also experience health problems like anxiety, depression, strokes, skin problems, digestion problems, etc.

We carry with us the memories of our angry outbursts for a very long time and suffer from frustration, guilt and depression.

Damages Relationships

As discussed previously, anger inhibits our ability to discern. As a result, we become more likely to use harsher tones and words, which can hurt those around us. Some of the things we say can be very difficult, if not impossible, for others to forget. Even if a relationship is not destroyed by such an incident, many are subtly marred by a moment's cruelty, never quite the same again.

Frequent angry outbursts between parents can have a lasting effect on children, who, when exposed to such flare-ups, tend to internalize the experiences. This ultimately leads to their developing anger issues as they grow older. In this way, the disease of anger spreads through generations, damaging the hearts of an ever-increasing number of people. We should consider the true impact our outbursts might have, not just on our immediate circle, but on future loved ones as well.

A Match in the Forest

We've already discussed how prolonged anger can gradually impair the body and mind, but the fact is, even a moment's indiscretion can spark a deadly fire that spreads beyond our control. A quick 'road rage' YouTube search will show you all you need to know about this phenomenon—you will find a small sample of the unlimited ocean of nightmarish, sometimes deadly, crashes that have occurred because of a driver's momentary lapse in anger management.

Triggers Wars

We have already seen how anger shuts off our intelligence and powers of discernment. When this happens to people in high positions, it can lead to wars.

Greece and Bulgaria had been at odds since the Balkan War of 1910. One day, when a Grecian soldier was chasing a dog, he crossed the border between the two countries, making Bulgarian soldiers angry. Later, they shot him, stoking the animosity of their rivals.

Greece immediately declared war, occupied a few villages of Bulgaria and tried to occupy a nearby city. Eventually, the international community intervened and called for a ceasefire, but not until both the countries lost many lives and spent a lot of money on war.

Heavy Financial Losses

A moment's indiscretion can lead to damaging not only cars but anything and everything around a person. Angry people often try to release their anger by throwing, punching, breaking or otherwise destroying things around them. This in turn may create a serious financial strain for whoever has to deal with the damaged property. Luddites were English weavers and textile workers of the nineteenth century. They were skilled workers. As the industrial revolution started introducing machines into every activity, including those of the textile industry, Luddites began losing their jobs and businesses, as machine-made products costed less than their handmade products. It became difficult for them to find jobs, as factories did not need many workers. This made Luddites frustrated and angry. They started a movement, destroying the machinery of textile mills and factories. The government used a lot of force to suppress the rebellion, but factory owners and the government had to experience heavy financial losses due to the destruction of machinery.

2.3. YOUR BRAIN AND BODY ON ANGER

We have already discussed how the parts of the brain are involved in responding to different kinds of situations: the amygdala is largely responsible for our emotional and behavioural responses—particularly those behaviours needed for survival, and when it senses danger, it immediately reacts and starts releasing hormones to prepare us to either fight or run to safety. The prefrontal cortex is responsible for planning, reasoning, controlling impulses and regulating emotions. These two components work together to help ensure our survival.

When something angers us, however, our amygdala bypasses the prefrontal cortex and takes us straight into 'fight' mode. Our breathing quickens, our heart starts pumping, adrenaline is released and our focus zeroes in on the source of our

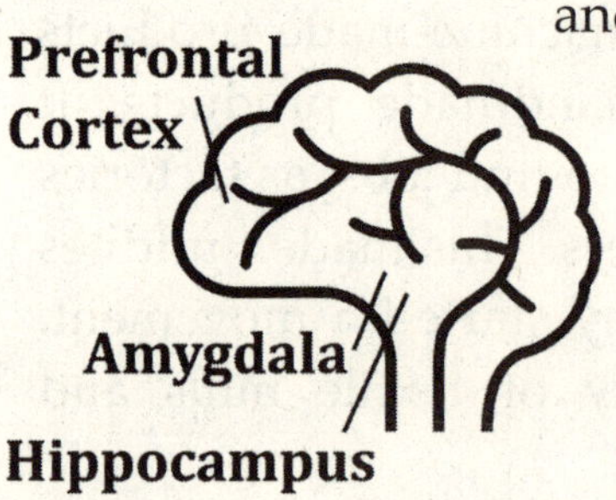

agitation. As a result of this internal intensity, we tend to say and do things that are impulsive, emotional and poorly reasoned. While such a reaction may have been helpful during historical periods when we were fighting others to the death for food, these days the 'amygdala hijack' tends to do more harm than good.

Within this phenomenon, however, lies the key to solving anger. By bypassing the amygdala instead of the cortex, we become more reasonable, sensible and empathetic. To do so, meditation techniques like deep breathing and mindfulness may be employed. Such techniques have been scientifically proven to shrink the amygdala and in turn diminish the anger we experience on a day-to-day basis.[1] In fact, by maintaining a strong spiritual foundation, one naturally increases one's empathy and respect for all those around one and thus decreases the likelihood of any kind of angry outburst. This will be more deeply explored in the sections to follow.

---

1 Kral, T., Schuyler, B. S., Mumford, J. A., Rosenkranz, M. A., Lutz, A., & Davidson, R. J. (2018). Impact of short- and long-term mindfulness meditation training on amygdala reactivity to emotional stimuli. *NeuroImage, 181*, 301–313.

The Tongue Has No Bones, But the Tongue Can Break Bones

Words have the power to hurt or heal others. If you blurt out words, you cannot take them back. It is like pressing the 'Send' button on older versions of email. You cannot undo it.

The tongue has no bones, but it can break bones. How? One way would be by overeating, but also by swearing and screaming at others. Most of the time, whatever feels good to the tongue is bad for the health of the body. If we start eating a lot of sugar because our tongue likes it, we might develop osteoporosis and our bones might become brittle and start breaking. If we hurt others with our words, they might initiate physical fights with us and hurt us.

How difficult is it to control the tongue? It is interesting to note that the tongue controls us the way the tiny tail of a fish controls the fish's movement. We can bring wild horses, lions and tigers under control. We can even charm a snake with music. But can we bring the human tongue under control? It is difficult. By overeating, we ruin our health. By speaking ill of or cursing others, we ruin our reputation and our physical wellbeing.

In the Ramayana, there is a story that is relevant in this regard. When Lord Rama was living in the forest with his wife Sita and his brother Lakshmana, a demoness by the name of Surpanaka happened to pass through their hermitage. When she saw Rama's beauty, she became infatuated and proposed to him. Rama told her that he was already married and had taken a vow of monogamy, but his brother Lakshmana, though married, was there without his wife, so he suggested she approach him instead. Lakshmana told her he was the servant of Rama and his wife Sita, and if Surpanaka wanted to marry him, she would have to become their servant as well.

Not realizing that they were simply making up excuses to avoid her, Surpanaka thought that although Rama liked her, he was rejecting her because of the presence of his beautiful wife Sita. Hence, she became angry with Sita and decided to kill her. She told Rama, 'Sita is the reason you are rejecting me. I can eat her alive and thus, both satisfy my tongue and permanently remove her from your life. We can then live together happily.' She even advanced towards Sita. Rama, realizing that danger was about to befall his wife, ordered Lakshmana to take action. Lakshmana punished Surpanaka and drove her away from their hermitage.

Surpanaka's tongue brought about not only her own ruination but also the ruination of her entire family in due time.

The sixteenth century poet Rupa Goswami said that if we can control our tongue, we can control our belly and genitals as well, as they are all in one line.[2]

Punished by Anger

We are all blissful beings by nature. Negative emotions like sadness, guilt and anger torment us, being unnatural. On a more physical level, science has found that anger and similar emotions also appear to be unnatural to the body, causing all kinds of ailments and diseases. The adrenaline and other chemicals released by the angry body take days to be fully flushed from the system, leaving the person who got angry feeling somewhat on edge long after they've reacted to the stimuli.

I know one successful man who would become angry at even the slightest transgressions by others. He would scream at and condemn others with violently abusive language. Eventually, despite his status, he developed a deep sense of loneliness, as

2 A.C. Bhaktivedanta Swami, *Nectar of Instruction* (Bhaktivedanta Book Trust, 1998).

no one wants to be around someone who is always on edge. He also became afflicted by various illnesses as a result of the stress he maintained in his body. In this way, he himself was punished by his excessive desire to punish others. Finally, coming to his senses, he realized the impact his anger was having and decided to change his ways. The next time you get angry, consider how your desire to harm someone else may actually harm you.

The Universality of Anger Management

All major religions condemn uncontrolled anger, regarding it as a gateway to despair. Let's consider a few powerful instances below that highlight this understanding.

One day, an angry man was yelling at Buddha. Unperturbed, Buddha asked him a question: 'If you try to give something to another person but they refuse it, what happens then?'

'I keep the thing with me,' said the angry man.

Buddha replied, 'The same is true of anger as well. If I don't take your words personally, they stay with you alone.'

> *Let every man be swift to hear, slow to speak, slow to wrath*. (James, 1:19–27)

> *Hot heads and cold hearts never solved a thing.* —Billy Graham.

> *He who is slow to anger is better than a strong man, and he who masters his passions is better than one who conquers a city*. (Proverbs 16:32)

> *A moment of patience within a moment of anger prevents a thousand moments of regret.*—Ali ibn Abi Talib

Suppression

Anger is an active emotion and its suppression can have serious repercussions. Think of what happens when someone twists the cap of a shaken soda bottle—BOOM! In the same way, it is only a matter of time before unprocessed anger causes us to erupt. Suppressed anger has also been known to cause depression and other mental disorders. Besides the mental toll it takes, suppressed anger can cause serious physical ailments as well.

In Korea, there is a serious disease called *hwabyung* that is caused by suppressed anger. Korean culture strongly emphasizes harmony, unity and social cohesion; as a result, many Koreans tend to push their negative emotions down instead of expressing them. When this suppression reaches a certain point, it triggers *hwabyung*, which causes burning sensations in the body, difficulty with breathing and other respiratory problems. It is not natural to suppress anger; rather, it should be *processed*.[3] By doing so, we will be able to avoid this volcano effect that causes problems both personally and with those around us.

3 Bou-Yong Rhi, 'Hwabyung—An Overview', *Psychiatry Investigation* 1(2004), pp. 21–24, https://www.psychiatryinvestigation.org/upload/pdf/0502004004.pdf

Explosion

The opposite of suppressing anger is to impulsively explode; an equally if not even more detrimental way of dealing with it. Even a slight provocation

can lead to exploders throwing things, screaming and sometimes even physically harming others. In its chronic form, this kind of anger manifests as Intermittent Explosive Disorder (IED), an ugly mental illness that often goes untreated. Most tend to try and simply tolerate intermittent exploders, but such outbursts require proper treatment. A failure to do so leads to loneliness, anguish, depression and physical harm. It is not normal to regularly bleed one's knuckles punching a wall. Any kind of chronic ailment that damages the body requires medical attention. Let's stop normalizing explosive anger and instead, give it the treatment it requires.

SUMMARY

Positive Aspects of Anger

Enables focus, awareness, self-defence and productivity, and wards off injustice.

Negative Aspects of Anger

Inhibits discrimination, depletes health, damages relationships and can lead to massive losses.

The Body's Reaction to Anger

The frontal lobe of the cortex is responsible for thinking, planning, memory and judgement. The amygdala identifies threats. When a threat is identified, the amygdala acts faster than the cortex and calls for action without considering potential consequences. The solution to anger management lies in training our brains to not bypass the cortex in the face of a provocation. Meditation, mindfulness and deep breathing help in this regard.

Both anger suppression and explosion breed various detrimental effects.

Questions

1. What were some of your recent experiences of anger? What were their negative and positive results?

___

___

___

___

2. What do you think are some ways of activating the cortex rather than the amygdala?

___

___

___

___

CHAPTER 3

Preventing Anger

Real manliness lies in shedding one's anger, the way the snake sheds its skin.

—Ramayana

3.1. THE THREE MODES OF MATERIAL NATURE

The laws of thermodynamics tell us that we can neither create nor destroy energy, but we can convert it from one form to another.

Nature's material energy is all-pervasive and acts on everyone in a very subtle way. We are surrounded by this energy. We call this 'material energy'.

What is this material energy? What is its power?

Why do we sometimes act against our will? Who or what is influencing us?

The force that impels us to act, sometimes against our own will, is this material energy, which has three modes. Since these modes have a captivating effect, they are considered subtle chains or ropes of nature. Based on how we act, we become either more or less influenced by a given mode. The influence of these modes is very subtle. Hence, we cannot see them, but we can perceive their influence on our actions. The Bhagavad Gita refers to them as the 'three modes of nature'—the mode of goodness (sattva), the mode of passion (rajas) and the mode of ignorance (tamas). They act on everyone in this world. It is important to recognize that 'goodness', 'passion' and 'ignorance' are technical words in this context and should not be understood in terms of their literal meanings.

Those in the mode of goodness, being naturally more calm and serene, are driven by their frontal cortex, which controls discernment and reason. They very rarely, if ever, experience the amygdala hijack phenomenon mentioned earlier. Those in the modes of passion and ignorance, however, being more impulsive, very frequently bypass their reasoning and impulsively react to provocations. Once their amygdala takes the wheel, it's all downhill from there.

This again highlights the importance of sattva. By engaging in spiritual practices like deep breathing and meditation, and by maintaining a regulated, balanced lifestyle, one naturally increases their sense of calm and awareness. In this state, one is much more likely to avoid anger's impulsive demands and instead exercise the power of prudence. With steady practice in developing this supreme state of mind, one can paint a beautiful landscape of life for oneself and others. Sattva is thus the key to becoming completely anger-free. We've alluded to a few changes we can make to increase the presence of sattva in our lives. Let us now take a deeper look at those changes.

1. Lifestyle
2. Thought processes
3. Discrimination
4. Motivations
5. Spirituality

3.2. LIFESTYLE

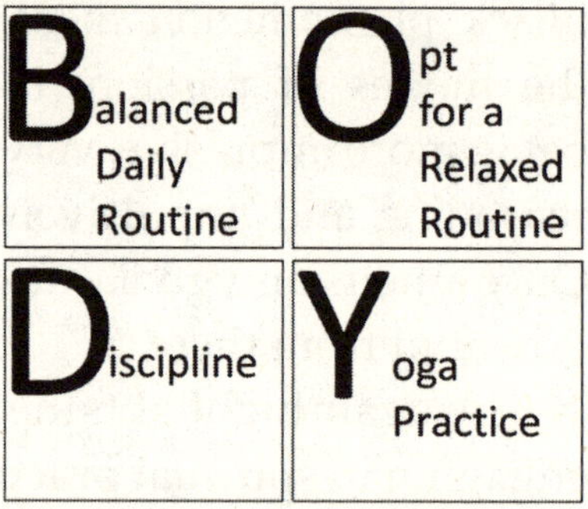

Our daily activities have a huge impact on the way we experience the world. This being the case, the way we arrange our life will dictate its quality. There are four key aspects to our lifestyle that we can tend to so as to ensure we experience optimal physiological conditions. I've broken them down using the acronym B.O.D.Y.

B—Balanced daily routine
O—Opt for a relaxed routine
D—Discipline
Y—Yoga practice

Let's now dive into each of these key components and see how we can fine-tune our lifestyle for an anger-free life.

Balanced Daily Routine

These days, everyone is busy, busy, busy. As soon as we open our eyes in the morning, we get on our phones and the rush begins. Getting ourselves ready, perhaps getting our kids ready, rushing them to school, then rushing to work ourselves, meeting tight deadlines, preparing meals, doing the laundry—the list goes on. By employing a daily routine, we enter into a kind of calm and steady flow instead of a perpetual mad dash. The Bhagavad Gita says that one who is regulated in their daily habits of eating, sleeping, recreation and work can mitigate all material pains.[4] To find such a balance amidst the clamour of modern life can certainly be a challenge, but with common sense and determination the flow can be found. Let us take a look at how we can balance some of these crucial components of our daily routine to achieve sustained tranquillity.

Balanced Eating

Eastern medicine declares digestion to be based on the movement of the sun. When the sun is at its peak, our digestive power peaks as well. The two then gradually decline in unison until midnight, when our digestive power bottoms out. Eating when our digestive power is diminished and not giving the body time to digest before sleeping can severely impair our rest, causing grogginess and irritability throughout the day. Instead, by eating our biggest meal at lunch (preferably

4 Bhagavad Gita (6.17)

around noon) and avoiding any sizable meals after dark, we avoid bogging our body down and thus preserve a more pristine mental state.

Just as important as when we eat is *how* we eat. Overeating leads to digestive difficulties, which in turn breed all kinds of diseases. Rather than stuffing ourselves to the brim, eastern medicine recommends we fill our stomach up about three-quarters and leave a fourth of empty space. Just as, when you fill a washing machine up to the brim, it doesn't work, over-stuffing your stomach will lead to some food not being properly digested. Instead, by eating only as much as feels comfortable (about three-fourths), we allow our body to digest all the food we consume and more fully extract nutrients from it.

Balanced Sleeping

As mentioned in the Time Management section, we should wind up all screen time about an hour before bed. This allows for deeper, more restful sleep, and in turn, more alert and active waking hours. Another aspect of sleep regulation is making sure one gets just the right amount. By sleeping too little, one deprives the body of much-needed replenishment; by oversleeping, the brain's release of serotonin is inhibited, which can lead to drowsiness, headaches and a slew of other chronic ailments. The solution is thus to gauge how many hours of sleep you need a night to be at your best, and as far as possible, to arrange your schedule so as to ensure you get them. By so doing, one may further optimize one's physical and mental wellness.

Balanced Recreation

Our recreation should be enlivening to the body, mind and soul. It should not be self-destructive or arbitrary. Those recreational activities that simply provide quick pleasure without any real substance appear like nectar at first but are just like poison in the end (think of the negative effects of intoxication). On the flipside, activities that may appear to be austere or even poisonous in the beginning often wind up being the most edifying and nectarine in the end. Some examples of this kind of recreation include reading spiritual books, practising yoga, practising mindfulness, doing meditation and spending time in nature. By relaxing in these ways, we not only enjoy the moment but set ourselves up for even deeper, more consistent peace and satisfaction down the line.

OPT FOR A RELAXED ROUTINE

Consider the body to be a machine. The mind is like the software that provides the directions to operate the hardware of the body. Overworking either one of these components will cause the whole system to fail. For this reason, we must be very conscious of the extent to which either is being overworked. After two hours of focusing on a project at work, take some time to let your mind cool down, perhaps go for a walk. When the body is feeling overworked, take time to relax, perhaps drink some cool water to recharge your batteries. When anger or frustration arises in the mind, slow down your breathing and rebalance your thinking.

Disciplined Lifestyle

As we've discussed, our mind and senses are impulsive. If we seek to fulfil each desire they present, we will end up on an endless despondent chase. Sensual pleasures may appear quite enjoyable, but in reality, most last for only a few moments before giving way to long-term anguish and dissatisfaction. For example, a severe diabetic who is addicted to sweets may give in to their urge, sacrificing their long-term health for a few moments' pleasure here and there. If someone denies the sensation such a pleasure-addict craves, the latter often responds in a crazed manner, lashing out at the person who dares to deny them their fill.

Many others try to scratch the itch for material enjoyment by taking intoxicants. They may know very well that the substance is not good for them, but due to a lack of discipline and fortitude in facing life's problems head-on, they give in. While such substances may appear to be helpful, in reality they only help us forget about our problems for a short time before thrusting us back into an even dimmer reality. While in an impaired mental state, many people also become more susceptible to angry outbursts, leaving an even grimmer reality for them to face when they finally come to—one in which their friends and family are growing increasingly tired of them.

A big part of avoiding anger is thus a strong level of self-discipline. Material cravings have the ability to manipulate us to act in angry, sometimes heinous ways that we would never have considered had we not been so desirous. These unnecessary cravings are products of the modes of passion and ignorance. By cultivating the mode of goodness through activities like meditation, mindfulness and tempered eating and sleeping, we can become less vulnerable to the influence of sense objects.

Yoga

Just as we service our car on a regular basis, we also need to service our body and mind. Practising yoga on a regular basis nourishes and replenishes the body just as regular oil changes replenish a car. Yoga is also a proven prophylactic for both physical ailments and mental infirmities like stress and depression. Regularly practising yogic breathing (pranayama) and yoga postures ultimately establishes us more deeply in the mode of goodness. It is ideal to perform yoga in the morning so as to set a sattvic tone for the day. Try practising a simple yoga flow like the sun salutation for just ten minutes a day and observe the difference you feel in your body, mind and spirit.

3.3. OUR THOUGHT PROCESS

Fifty to sixty thousand thoughts pass through our mind in a single day. The kinds of thoughts that occupy our brain are thus incredibly powerful. This is especially pertinent in the context of anger management; anger originates from the mind and thus, the way to uproot it resides therein. Let's explore some prudent information about the mind and its connection to who we are and what we do.

A Basic Overview of Mind, Body and Intelligence

Our body can be compared to a chariot. Our five senses (sight, smell, sound, taste and touch) are five wild horses pulling the chariot in different directions. Our mind represents the reins. Our intelligence is the driver and the passenger is the soul. If the charioteer holds the reins tightly and controls the horses, the passenger safely reaches the destination. In other words, if we intelligently guide our senses (instead of letting *them* pull *us* around) we will reach our desired destination. If, instead, we allow the senses to run wild, we'll be pulled in every which way, ever dissatisfied.

By nature, the senses are pleasure-seeking and pain-avoiding. If we let them run the show, we'll be pulled towards experiences that may give us some short-term pleasure but will not provide the inner satisfaction and solace that the soul truly craves. Those who wholly abide by the idea of 'having a good time' generally end up addicted to pleasurable substances and out of work; after all, going to work isn't always a blissful experience. We need to resist the pull of the senses and instead engage in activities that bring the soul joy, not just the body. By using our intelligence to discern between hollow happiness and long-term satisfaction, we can avoid the unnecessary anger caused by insatiable desires and live in a state of true, well-discerned happiness that doesn't depend on any external thing.

Bad Vibrations: The Mind's Transmissions

Anger doesn't always manifest through words or actions. The mind is so powerful that it can express discontent even without recourse to these overt expressions. It is a transmitter and receiver. Imagine yourself entering a party at which, for some reason, most of the people present dislike you. Immediately, you are hit by their vibes as you step in. Can you feel the awkwardness or uneasiness? The dissatisfaction in the air? Based on the state of mind of the attendees, your mind will be able to tell you that you're not welcome without a word having been said. People harbour negative feelings towards each other all the time. This causes them to be blocked off from one another by the iron wall of negativity and subtle anger.

Whenever we feel we are brewing feelings of discontentment towards someone, especially a family member or a colleague, we should promptly address the problem. By simply expressing ourselves in a genuine way, explaining to the person what they did and how it made us feel without attacking them for it, we might be able to ultimately save the relationship. By failing to do so, we doom our connection to an ever-increasing state of awkward bitterness. Harboured anger is like a viral disease; if left untreated, it will simply grow stronger. Snuff out the negativity in your heart by sharing your feelings with the person you feel it towards and cure yourself of the dreaded disease once and for all.

Killing Anger with Humour

When the fire of anger begins brewing in someone's heart, sometimes the most effective thing we can do is douse it with the cool water of humour. Humour can relieve the tension of a given situation by showing the other person that we are not angry with

them, even if they are with us. Socrates, the brilliant philosopher, was apparently an expert at this—especially in his personal dealings. Annoyed at the constant presence of his disciples at their home due to Socrates' insistence on holding lectures there, his wife Xanthippe one day began harshly attacking the philosopher with thunderous words. She became so enraged that she dumped a whole bucket of water on him. Socrates finally replied, 'Well, after thunder comes the rain.' He thus defused the situation instead of letting it escalate further.

Socrates once remarked that anger makes beasts out of men. As seen here, humour is a decidedly human characteristic that can both calm and reverse the emotions of a heated situation. It also caters to our innate desire to enjoy, thus further relieving tensions caused by the fact of that desire being blocked in some way. Instead of responding with more anger, consider employing a little humour the next time you find yourself in a heated situation. After all, fire can't be subdued with more fire; try some water instead.

Feed the Good Dog

How can we cultivate a more serene state of mind? In this connection, there is a Cherokee

Nation story about two quarrelling dogs—one good and one bad. The good dog is the part of us that imbibes qualities like humility, tolerance, patience, love and so on. The bad dog is the part that imbibes qualities like anger, lust, greed, envy, pride, etc. It is said that these dogs are in a constant battle for supremacy. So, which one will come out victorious? Well, it's simple—the one we feed. In other words, whichever qualities we consciously cultivate will become more prevalent, while those that we vigilantly avoid will gradually diminish.

While this may sound simple, to actually alter the way we think about and react to things in our day-to-day life can be quite a challenge. Our thoughts are generally products of our past experiences. We've been conditioned to think and act in certain ways. Each time we give in to those conditioned ways, we strengthen their grip on us. By changing our thinking and thus the way we act, we gradually break old habits and form new ones. So the question then becomes: how can one change one's way of thinking so as to imbibe more good qualities and shed bad ones? For this, there are a few tried and true techniques that we can employ for definite results. Let's take a look at a few.

Overcoming Negativity

The writer John Milton wrote in *Paradise Lost*, 'The mind is its own place and in itself can make a heaven of hell or a hell of heaven.' Have you ever stopped to think about how your thoughts manipulate your emotions? We might be in the greatest place in the world, but if we are worried about some pressing matter, even paradise can appear hellish. From time to time, we all experience states in which our minds latch on to continuous streams of negative thoughts. Perhaps you can relate to hearing some of the following put-downs that the mind tends to throw at us in dark times:

'I am good for nothing.'

'Everyone else is happy.'

'No one else has to deal with the problems that I have to deal with.'

'I've achieved nothing.'

'My life is useless.'

'I can't believe I did that.'

'What if I don't amount to anything?'

'Nothing makes me happy.'

'I'm incompetent.'

Everyone deals with these types of thoughts from time to time, even the most apparently successful amongst us. Once, a PhD student from Carnegie Mellon University came to me depressed. He began explaining to me how useless he felt and how it seemed that problems chased after him wherever he went. He was particularly disappointed about not being as far along with his studies as he would have liked.

I told him, 'You are a performer. You have graduated from a top-notch university already and now you are earning a PhD at one of the best universities in America! Just because the results are not coming in within the exact timeframe you expected does not mean you should feel bad.' He appreciated this perspective and began to consider how detrimental a negative thought process can be to one's prosperity. Since then, we've met regularly and worked together to combat these thoughts with great success. He has now finished his PhD and leads a successful life.

There are seven specific techniques I employed to help turn his mindset around for good. Let's take a look at them and see how we may be able to apply them to our own unique situations.

1. Remember and realize:
   a. *You* are not the mind or the body. You are stronger, smarter and braver than you think.
   b. Every problem is temporary.
   c. You are powerful and can both do and undo things.
   d. An uncontrolled mind is your worst enemy. Handle it carefully.
2. Recognize and ignore negative thoughts.

   Unwanted thoughts are like unwanted pests; if you don't feed them, they won't stay for long. If a certain thought comes up again and again, it means you have some interest in it. Instead of engaging with such thoughts, just observe them and the negative effect they have on you; observe them and watch them float by without reacting to them. Develop the tendency of neglecting the thoughts that weigh you down.

3. Replace negative thoughts with positive ones.

   It is not possible to simply delete things from our minds; we can only replace them. Try replacing the negative thoughts you're having with positive ones. Each time the mind presents some limiting belief or conception, replace it with an empowering one. Replace negative self-talk with positive self-talk. Because our thoughts eventually become our actions, developing a positive state of mind will eventually translate into a positive lifestyle. By so doing, we will shine a warm light on those around us instead of a cold, angry one.

4. Don't sit idle.

   Sometimes we feel we can't stop the flow of negative thoughts no matter how hard we try. Giving in to the negative pressure, we often become paralysed by it, overwhelmed by a sense of incompetence and despondence. In such situations, silent meditation can worsen the dilemma as one only becomes even more aware of the negativity brewing within. The best remedy is to get active. Try doing something productive, even something small, and thus build a ladder out of the hole you've fallen into. Alternatively, you can have a positive conversation with someone dear to you so as to relieve the mounting mental pressure that a closed-off mind creates.

5. Remember your strengths and achievements.

   Take a moment to think of the high points of your life and remember your dormant potential for success. These recollections could be simple: the spelling bee victory, the Little League home run, that time when you finally landed the job you were after, etc. Just remember at least one instance in which you were commended for your successful efforts. This can give you enough of a push to start moving forward.

6. Practise mantra meditation.

   Meditation is a very effective way of overcoming negative thoughts. Through meditation, you become a witness to the world within instead of a victim of it. Meditation thus helps separate us from the endless stream of thoughts that dictate how we feel. While there are various types of meditation, mantra meditation is considered the most powerful way to control the mind. In Vedic literature, it is said that 'Man' means mind, 'tra' means to liberate. Mantra is thus an ancient sound vibration that carries the power to liberate us from the mind's pulling. By becoming thus liberated, we can take back control of our mind and use it for our ultimate good. With regular practice, mantra meditation will slowly transfer this power to us.

7. Reveal your problems to loved ones or to a counsellor.

   Share your problem before it's too late. In oriental traditions, there is a famous saying: 'Happiness, when shared with others, increases. Distress, when shared with others, decreases.' We should express ourselves—the feelings in our hearts—to those near and dear to us and thus begin healing our wounds. Sharing our problems with dear ones lifts the mind's burden. We feel refreshed as we receive support from those who have a sincere desire to help.

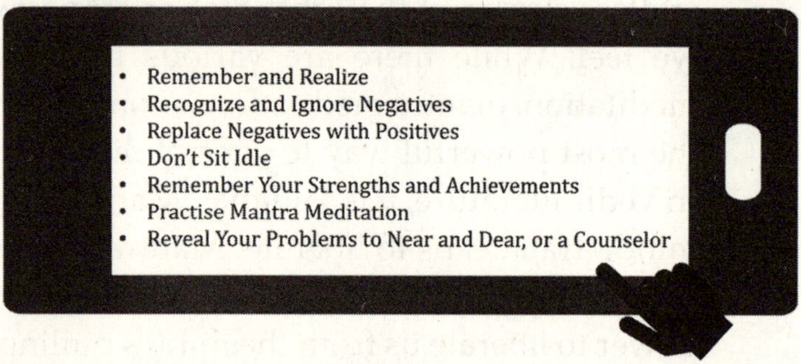

3.4. POWER OF JUDGEMENT

As mentioned previously, the mind is impulsive. Our intelligence, however, is known for its astute judgement. Our intelligence should be trained to deeply consider anger's consequences, particularly at times when the mind is boiling with anger. While altering angry habits is near impossible in the heat of the moment, we can pre-emptively train ourselves in cooler times so that when the heat arises, we are prepared. Make a routine of considering anger's ill effects—how it breaks the heart of one's spouse, saddens one's family members, mars one's reputation and harms one's body. Consider the consequences that previous outbursts have produced—strained relationships, monetary losses, legal issues, whatever they may be. Take time to reflect upon all the pain anger brings. Finally, think about the wisest way of dealing with similarly incendiary situations going forward. In this way, develop a 'growth mindset' that will allow you to learn from past mistakes and train yourself to prevent their recurrence.

Channel Anger for Long-term Success

As we now know, anger triggers the release of catecholamines that energize the body for impassioned action. Instead of aiming this energy at others, it is better to channel it into actions that will prevent the triggering situation from arising in the future. Consider the following example in this regard.

Once, in East Asia, a large group of shoe factory workers requested a reasonable raise. Despite repeated requests, their management remained unmoved. This infuriated the workers, who were left with a choice between leaving the company or going on strike. Instead, they came up with a third option. Each decided to work extra hours and generate twice as much output for the company. Within a couple of months, their management realized the enormous output increase and finally relented to the workers' demands. This can be likened to Gandhi's non-violence movement, which channelled the same anger in a productive way that ultimately led to India's freedom. How can you channel the anger produced by recurring situations into work that will prevent their recurrence?

3.5. MOTIVES BEHIND ACTIONS: EGO OR SERVICE (INTROSPECTION)

One of our internal anger triggers is the 'I am the doer' mentality.

If we have an 'I am the doer' mentality, we naturally develop a controlling nature. When things don't go our way, we become angry. If we keep becoming angry at people around us, we eventually lose them. We must ask these questions all the time:

Am I serving my ego or am I serving others?

(or)

What is *actually* driving me to perform my actions?

When the ego is not driving us to perform our actions, a service attitude will. This will eventually make us selfless and grateful.

If our motive is to serve our ego, we will eventually be frustrated. But if we are motivated to serve the people around us, we will receive grace.

Our endeavour is not enough. We need the sanction of God to accomplish anything. Everything, including our temporary body, comes from nature.

We only manipulate nature's resources. If we understand this, we also understand the need to be humble. This world is designed in such a way that we either become voluntarily humble or get humbled by nature as a result of various situations in our life.

Usually, humble people do not become angry and they are also very forgiving. If you hone these principles in your life, you will make lot of progress.

3.6. OUR SPIRITUALITY

How does spirituality help reduce anger?

Spirituality starts with the understanding that we are not the body or the mind, that we are the spirit soul within. As previously mentioned, the modes of nature wield an influence over our body and mind, triggering qualities like anger, envy, greed, etc. By cultivating spirituality, we transcend the body and mind and thus the influence the modes of nature have upon us. As the transcendental process continues, we gain knowledge of the world around us and detach ourselves from its causes and effects. At this stage, we then exert strong control over all of our emotions, especially anger.

How do we develop our spirituality?

Before we discuss spirituality any further, let us discuss the terms IQ, EQ and SQ.

IQ

Intelligence quotient is a measure of one's ability to reason. People with high IQ typically have better memory, reasoning abilities and greater capacities to effectively process information and generate results.

EQ

Emotional quotient is a measure of one's ability to relate to others. Another term for this is emotional intelligence. People with high EQ are aware of their emotions and those of others. They also possess the ability to comfortably connect with others in a way that forges strong bonds.

SQ

Spiritual quotient is a measure of one's ability to discern and act upon the meaning of life. SQ empowers us to be creative, reflective, inquisitive and introspective. It helps us determine the more substantial aspects of life and thus realize our fullest human potential. A person with a high SQ carefully discerns between right and wrong and is naturally determined to act with integrity.

Paul Chippendale further explains SQ as follows:

> Spiritual intelligence could also be called the 'intelligence of meaning'. It is what makes us essentially human—the ability to plan, to make sense of our emotions, to control our impulses, to make choices, and to endow our world with meaning. The frontal lobes of the brain are where our ideas are created; where plans are constructed; thoughts joined with their associations to form new memories; and fleeting perceptions are held in mind until they are dispatched to long-term memory or to oblivion.[5]

Our spiritual quotient gives us the power to not only tell the difference between right and wrong, but also to curb our impulses when they arise. SQ is ultimately the key to taming anger.

In spiritual circles, many people are trained to develop SQ with the A.B.C.D. formula:

---

5 Chippendale, P. (2001). *Our Three Main Intelligences*. Minessence Group.

A–Association with high-minded people

B–Books (wisdom books)

C–Chant for change (mantra meditation)

D–Diet (eating karma-free vegetarian food)

Now let us go a bit deeper into each aspect of the formula:

Association with high-minded people

Scriptures emphasize the importance of associating with sages and saints. But how do we know who is a sage or a saint? Who are spiritual people? What are their qualities? The Bhagavat Purana, an ancient scripture, mentions that sages are tolerant, merciful and friendly to all living entities.[6] They have no enemies; they are peaceful and guided by scriptures. If you find anyone with these qualities, you have found a sage to associate with!

We need to discuss spiritual topics with sages and spiritual people. This kind of interaction clears the mind of misconceptions and illuminates important angles of vision that we may not have been aware of before. Such spiritually-minded people are conscious of the temporality of the

6 Srimad Bhagavatam (3.25.21)

body. At the same time, they're also conscious of the fact that the soul is eternal. Acknowledging these two contrasting considerations, such people dedicate their lives to solving life's biggest problems. Their broad vision makes them immune to the petty issues of materialistic life. Simply by associating with such personalities, we too can overcome life's petty naggings by way of a broader perspective. Just as an iron rod becomes red hot in its association with fire, we too become sources of light and warmth by associating with those who exude such qualities.

Books

Reading spiritual books sharpens our understanding of the ultimate goals of life and how we may work towards them. Even fifteen minutes a day spent immersing our consciousness in something sublime can have incredible effects. By regularly focusing on topics like the soul, the ego, the mind, the modes of nature and the like, we can start to view the world through a very different lens. Developing the right lens, a spiritual lens, can completely change the way we respond to stimuli in our environment, and we might end up leading a more balanced and controlled life.

Chant

As previously mentioned, mantra meditation is specifically endowed with the power to curb the negative and restless mind. When we engage in this practice, we soften the harshness of the external world and operate more smoothly within it. The benefits are practically endless. We will go deeper into its immense power in the following chapter.

Diet

The Bhagavad Gita declares vegetarian food to belong to the mode of goodness. Such food helps orient our mind to a more peaceful state of being. Overly spicy or pungent food is linked to the mode of passion and animal flesh to the mode of ignorance. Such foods put us in a restless or depressed state of mind, inhibiting our potential to achieve lasting peace and satisfaction. Eating meat has been found to be unnatural for humans in more recent years. Biologists and dieticians have studied the anatomical differences between carnivores and herbivores compared to humans and found that our bodies are naturally suited to a plant-based diet.

As presented in the above table, we find that the teeth of carnivorous animals are designed to tear flesh and immediately swallow it, whereas human teeth are designed to chew food that is less tough and to slowly digest it. Carnivorous saliva and stomach acid are very acidic, so as to powerfully break down the flesh they swallow. Their intestines are also short, so it is easy for them to promptly excrete what they can't digest. Humans and herbivores have molars to chew their food. Our intestines are long and curvy, with pockets, in order to allow us to slowly absorb nutrients from plants and fruits. This length and curviness means that undigested meat rots in our body, releasing toxins and causing diseases, the most common resulting ailment being heart disease, the leading cause of death worldwide.[7]

Besides heart disease, type 2 diabetes and cancer, a subtler disease of the heart is also caused by meat-eating. As Socrates put it, 'Don't talk of love and peace with a dead animal on your plate.' He, Benjamin Franklin, Mahatma Gandhi and many of the most productive, impactful and peaceful people in the world practised vegetarianism. Consuming only those foods that are conducive to the mode of goodness will result in anger born of

---

7 World Health Organization. (2020). *The Top 10 Causes of Death*. WHO.

Organ	Carnivorous Animals	Herbivorous Animals	Humans
Small intestine	3 to 5 times body length	>10 times body length	>10 times body length
Bowels	Simple, smooth and short	Long, bumpy and full of pockets	Long, curvy, bumpy and full of pockets
Acid in stomach	PH < 1	PH = 4 or 5	PH = 4 or 5
Saliva	Acidic	Alkaline	Alkaline
Canine teeth	Sharp and curved	Dull and short	Short and blunt
Fingernails	Sharp claws	Usually absent	Short and soft
Fibre	Don't need fibre	Need fibre	Need fibre
Teeth	No flat molar teeth for chewing	Flat molar teeth for chewing	Flat molar teeth for chewing

passion and ignorance being far less prevalent in one's heart and mind.

By practising the A.B.C.D. method, one can develop one's spiritual intelligence and thus becomes gradually more aloof from the pangs of the uncontrolled mind. In such a state, all negative qualities like anger, greed, envy and avarice are progressively subdued. One thus regains control of their emotional state of being, and ultimately, their life.

The More You Know ...

Sometimes, in our dreams, we may see a tiger chasing us and become entrapped by fear, as if we were truly being hunted in real life. Similarly, sometimes children become engrossed in the fight scene of a movie, rising and throwing their fists around as if they themselves were the hero. Sometimes adults do the same thing, breaking down in tears at the final scene of a movie as a result of deeply identifying with the characters therein. However, all such forms of identification are illusory and temporary experiences. In a similar way, we, as pure spirit souls, falsely identify with the body and its experiences of happiness and distress. Actually, as spirits, we are beyond all these ups and downs. As souls, we are born with the right to experience bliss.

You may find, upon consideration, that all forms of happiness and distress in this world are short-lived. In the Bhagavad Gita, Krishna says, 'The non-permanent appearance of happiness and distress, and their disappearance in due course, are like the appearance and disappearance of winter and summer seasons. They arise from sense perception, and one must learn to tolerate them without being disturbed.'[8] Rather than becoming overly disturbed by a particular mishap, we should remain tolerant, understanding both the temporariness and inevitability of distressing conditions in this world. By acting based on knowledge, instead of emotion, we can avoid anger's grip and remain just above the endless fray of illusory miseries.

Both happiness and distress are short-lived in this world. There is no permanent happiness or permanent distress here. All feelings of happiness and distress are due to our sense perception.

Usually, young models present products in advertisements to impress upon the viewer that purchasing that product will make them happy. If we think a product will give us pleasure, we go for

8 Bhagavad Gita (2.14)

it. But experience has proved that all the sensual pleasures of this world are very short-lived. The Gita says that these sensory pleasures and pains are dependent on the imagination. A person may be enjoying a cigarette in a room while another person in the same room may be miserable because of the smoke. It is all based on sense perception.

If we understand these facts, they will help us work on our behaviour. When I was infected by COVID-19 along with a few others in our monastery, all of us were extremely careful—except for one person. He did not care to wear a mask. Someone told him that this sickness was just a cough and would go away in a few days. This led me to understand the importance of knowledge and acting based on knowledge. This is true with anger management as well. When we lead our lives based on knowledge and truth, our lives become better.

Develop Divine Qualities

According to the ancient wisdom texts, we are spirit souls and cannot be reduced to the physical body or subtle mind. The nature of the soul is to be happy. Since we are stuck in this body, we forgot we are spirit souls and we try to derive happiness through the mind and senses, which is a very low level of happiness and not a long-lasting one. We do this because we are not aware of the unlimited pleasure of the self. It is exceedingly rare for a soul to take birth as a human being, out of all the millions of species of life available. Human life grants us the unique opportunity to be able to understand our unnatural sojourn here as spiritual beings in the material world. It affords us the opportunity to transcend lower qualities like anger and attain a divine state of being made up of qualities like patience, tolerance and love. In this state, we not only give up anger but accept a position of pure joy and satisfaction. Developing divine qualities using the A.B.C.D. method and cultivating spiritual knowledge lead to all undesirable qualities naturally falling away, just as one may drop a penny in the process of picking up a hundred-dollar bill.

SUMMARY

- Nature influences us through the three modes: goodness, passion and ignorance
- The mode of goodness leads to tranquillity and progress
- The mode of passion leads to mixed results
- The mode of ignorance leads to misery

By becoming situated in the mode of goodness, we enable the development in ourselves of the mentality required to tolerate provocative situations and abstain from indulging in anger.

Physical Lifestyle

- Adopt a balanced way of eating, sleeping and recreating
- Stay away from stimulants and intoxicants and illicit relationships and lead a disciplined life

Thought Process

- Maintain a sense of humour
- Cultivate positive thoughts and neglect negative ones
- Practise meditation
- Share your thoughts with trustworthy people

Power of Discrimination

- Use angry energy to solve problems instead of prolonging them

Motives behind Our Actions

- Find happiness in serving, not in controlling others

- A controlling mentality makes us miserable

Spirituality

Follow the A.B.C.D. formula:

A–Association with high-minded people

B–Books (wisdom books)

C–Chant (mantra meditation)

D–Diet (eating karma-free vegetarian food)

Questions

1. What steps will you take on a physical level to curb your anger?

____

____

____

____

2. What is the relationship between the soul on the one hand and the body and mind on the other?

____

____

3. What steps will you take to realize your inner strength and potential?

4. What little services can you perform to keep people around you happy?

5. What internal steps will you take to cultivate positivity?

CHAPTER 4

Anger Management Techniques

4.1. STRATEGIES TO COPE WITH ANGER

Upon becoming angry, we must learn to safely release the pent-up pressure in a safe way. To this end, we may employ the S.A.M.P.L.E. formula:

S–Shift your focus

A–Attain soul space

M–Mantra meditation

P–Pranayama

L–Listen to uplifting sounds

E–Escape provocation

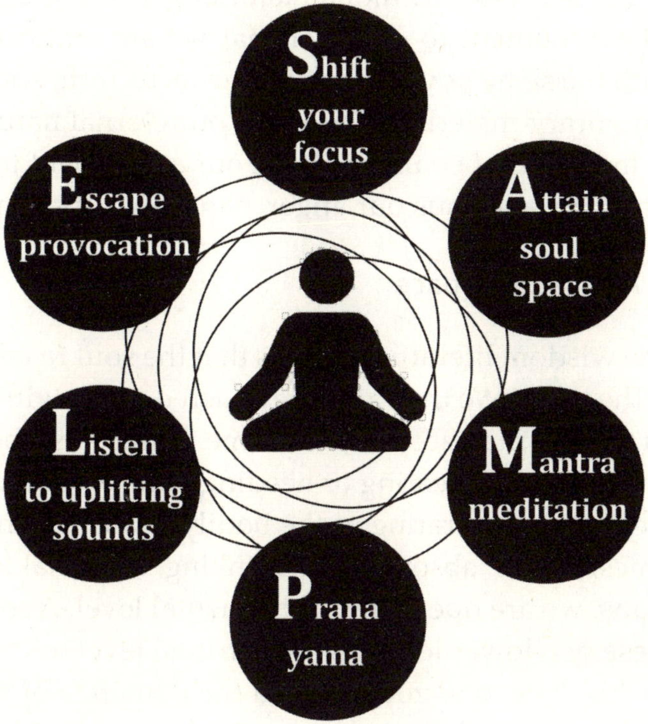

S: Shift Your Focus

As soon as we sense our anger mounting, instead of dwelling on its cause, we should shift our focus to something else. If someone offends us at the level of our body or mind, we should remember that we, as souls, are neither of those things. As souls, we are full of pure, illuminating energy, just like the sun. The sun is the most powerful source of energy in the universe; in moments of anger, we should take a moment to consider that we are endowed with the same power. Shifting the focus from some temporary material hang-up to our eternal nature as magnificent souls results in our attachment to a situation, and thus our anger, naturally subsiding.

A: Attain Soul Space

The wisdom literature tells us that the soul resides in the heart. We thus all have a sacred space within us that we may access at any time. While absorbed in activities like eating or heeding nature's call, we are usually operating at the bodily level. At other times, while absorbed in thinking and making plans, we are operating at the mental level. Above these two lower levels is the spiritual level within. In this state, one goes beyond the demands of the body and mind, finding a peaceful refuge from all anxieties. In fact, sages in the past would engage in intense spiritual practices to remain in the soul space and experience immense joy. Some yogis who are adept in reaching soul space effortlessly and freely wander the Himalayan mountains during frigid winters with very little clothes on. The methods that constitute the rest of the S.A.M.P.L.E. formula allow one to situate oneself in the soul space.

M: Mantra Meditation

As discussed earlier, mantras are sacred hymns that liberate one from the pulls of the mind. This technique is practised by millions around the world as a means of entering deeply the soul space on a regular basis. Regular mantra meditation helps to disconnect from the agitations of the body and mind. Invoking mantras in times of distress has also proved to be a powerful way of subduing one's emotions. Through both regular practice and the practice of calling upon our mantras in times of need, we will be able to feel the grip of anger and impulsivity gradually loosen.

P: Pranayama Breathing Technique

When anger arises, breathing quickens. Ancient yogis and now modern scientists have found that there is an interesting relationship between the breath and the mental state. While it is obvious that emotions wield an influence over breathing, a less-known fact is that breathing also wields power over emotions. Regulating our breath will allow us to regulate our mental condition. This ancient art of breath regulation goes by the name of pranayama. Try out the following step-by-step process and see how your mind and heart respond.

1. Slowly fill the lungs with air.
2. Hold your breath for a few moments.
3. Slowly empty the lungs of air.
4. Hold your breath for a few moments.
5. Repeat.

While the intricacies of pranayama are many, this simple version provides a foundation that you may build upon and utilize in your day-to-day life for immediate results.

L: Listen to Uplifting Sounds

When anger gets us down, sometimes even a single word from a spiritually-realized person can yank us out of the rut. Sometimes we need only to be reminded of the supreme value of qualities like tolerance, humility, compassion and selflessness to be empowered to let go of our negativity. Spiritual music or kirtan yoga also has a special effect on the mind, allowing it to release anger in a harmless way. These kinds of spiritual sound vibrations penetrate the outer coverings of the mind and heart and reignite the light of the blissful soul. Listening to/watching comedic content is also a useful option.

E: Escape the Situation

> *Any person capable of angering you becomes your master; he can anger you only when you allow yourself to be disturbed by him.*
>
> —Epictetus

Getting out of a potentially angering situation is sometimes the safest way of saving the day. As soon as we sense some sharpness in the voice of the opposite party, the best option for us is often to promptly excuse ourselves from the scene. While walking away, take long deep breaths to quell any desire to respond that may be brewing within. If possible, walk to an open, outdoor space and take in some fresh air. By taking the high road out of there, we practically eliminate the possibility of any escalation. Also, it is better to avoid getting into arguments at parties and meetings, especially with unknown people.

4.2. BAD MOODS: RECOGNIZE AND RESPOND

Most people find it impossible to be happy all the time. Disturbances are inevitable. No matter how hard we try to stay in high spirits, circumstances will always arise that put us in a sour state of mind. Though we may not necessarily be in an *angry* mood, a bad mood of any sort often leads to anger. This being the case, we must learn to recognize these bad moods in ourselves and others and respond in such a way that the latent anger present is not stoked.

4.3. IDENTIFY TRIGGERS AND WARNING SIGNS OF A BAD MOOD

Humiliation

Humiliation causes people to be on edge due to the way the ego operates. They tend to go searching for a way to regain their pride by humiliating someone else. If we find ourselves affected by this mental state, we can practise pranayama and/or mantra meditation, go for a long walk or just take some time to be alone and regain composure. Otherwise, any person we meet can become a stepping stone towards avenging our humiliation.

There is a pertinent story from the Mahabharata in this connection. During the Kurukshetra battle, the warrior Karna defeated another warrior, Dharma, and humiliated him with scornful words. Upon hearing of his friend Dharma's defeat, the illustrious warrior Arjuna rushed to their encampment to check on him. At the sight of Arjuna, Dharma became elated, thinking Arjuna had defeated Karna. But he found out instead that Arjuna had not even yet faced Karna, became enraged and demeaned Arjuna with harsh words. This is an example of circumstantial anger. When we find ourselves in Arjuna's position, we should not take seriously the insults of our aggressor, knowing well their impaired state of mind.[9]

Lack of Sleep

The mind needs adequate rest to properly function. When we don't get enough sleep, our mind fails to fully recover from the previous night's fatigue and thus becomes restless. If anyone disturbs us even slightly, we become inordinately upset and subject them to harsh words. When we find ourselves in this state, we should take a break from whatever we are doing and sleep, or at least rest for some time. When we notice others in a sleep-deprived state, we should recognize their impaired condition and not take personally any heat they may direct our way.

Stress

If we are overburdened at work or have hard deadlines approaching, we might naturally

9 Mahabharata Karna Parva

experience some stress. Going through prolonged problems of any sort causes stress. During severely stressful situations, we become restless. This releases adrenaline into the body to help maintain our heartbeat and blood pressure. Due to this, we are naturally a bit more on edge and thus more prone to losing our temper. Children and other family members should take note of this point. When the parents are stressed out due to work or other reasons, they should not be disturbed with trivial problems.

Exhaustion

When people return home from work, they are usually exhausted, having taxed their body and mind the entire day. Exhaustion brings about a bad mood. It is one of the reasons for road rage. This is a common problem if everyone in the family works. If someone irritates you while you are in that state, it is likely that you will get provoked and become angry. When you find that you are exhausted, take a bath and a power nap to recover from the fatigue.

Failure and Rejection

Failure spoils moods. When we fail to properly perform or are rejected, we get into a bad mood.

When we can't meet our own expectations or those of our parents, bad moods take over. At this time, we need to talk to someone who can inspire us and lift our spirits. That is why it is important to have good relationships with people so that we can share our concerns with them. Otherwise, bad moods prevail.

Hunger

Hunger also triggers bad moods. I've seen many people become angry due to the body's demands. When hunger teams up with exhaustion, anger is nearly inevitable. In such situations, we should avoid speaking until we eat.

4.4. HOW TO RECOVER FROM A BAD MOOD

When we realize our mood has been spoilt, we need to be able to snap out of it. Below are a few ways to stabilize emotions and enter into a more positive state of mind.

1. Remember the good times you have had and achievements you are proud of.
2. Listen to inspirational lectures.
3. Learn from your mistakes and move forward.

4. Remember that it's not the end of the world.
5. Read spiritual books.
6. Engage in some constructive activity.
7. Pray.
8. Practise yoga.
9. Practise meditation.
10. Rest.
11. Exchange humour.

As spiritual souls, we are very powerful. We have the ability to change the way we feel at any given moment. If we genuinely desire to heal our state of mind, we may take the steps necessary to do so. We need only have the will power to actively perform some of these activities instead of getting upset. By so doing and by learning from our bad moods instead of just letting them have their way with us, we can move ahead, into a more relaxed and satisfied state. One point to note here is that when our mental state is compromised, we should not engage in important conversations and arguments. If we cannot avoid them, we should be careful while speaking.

4.5. TASTE WHAT YOU'RE COOKING BEFORE YOU SERVE IT

The words of the reckless pierce like swords, but the tongues of the wise bring healing.

– Proverbs 12:18

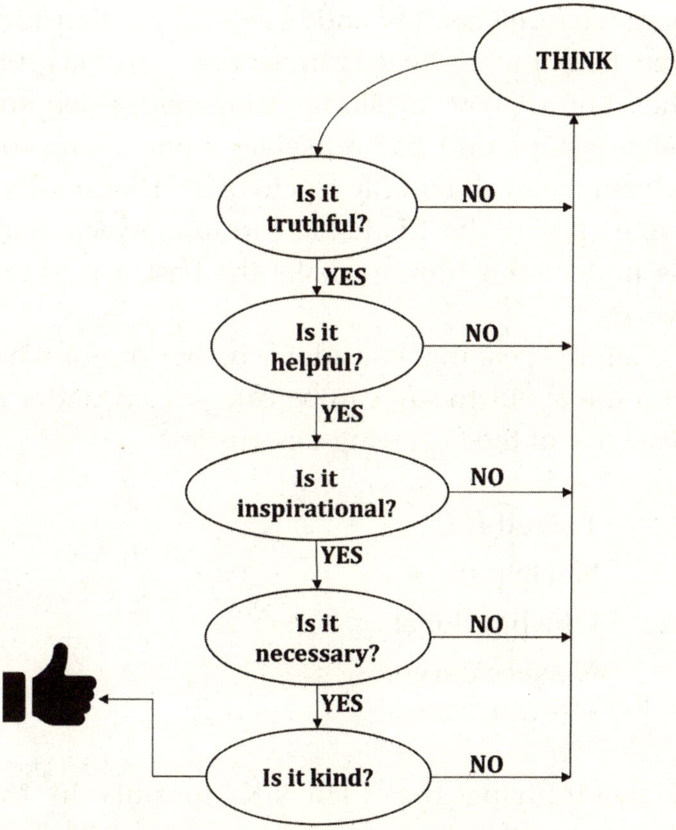

Our words have the power to deeply hurt or deeply heal. We need to be mindful of how we use them. You must have come across the famous saying 'Think twice before you speak'. But how often do we actually consider our thoughts before allowing them to manifest as words? Words play a vital role in our overall prosperity. By speaking in a conscious way, we forge healthy and beneficial relationships that help put us in advantageous positions. On the contrary, by speaking belligerently, we soil relationships and bar ourselves from taking full advantage of all that life has to offer. That is why I came up with the T.H.I.N.K. formula, which helps us understand how to make the best use of our words.

Before speaking, consider whether or not what you are about to say can be categorized under at least one of the following descriptors:

T–Truthful

H–Helpful

I–Inspirational

N–Necessary

K–Kind

By applying the T.H.I.N.K. formula in our dealings with others, we can avoid the pitfalls of angry speech and thus more easily forge healthy relationships with those around us.

4.6. 7–38–55 RULE

Communication isn't all about speech. According to Dr Albert Mehrabian, Professor Emeritus of Psychology at the University of California, Los Angeles, 55 per cent of communication is based on one's body language, 38 per cent on one's tone of voice and only 7per cent on the actual words one speaks. Things like body language and tone of voice depend upon one's mood and mentality. While our words may attempt to hide these things, they inevitably show themselves whether we want them to or not. Thus, in our attempts to communicate in a non-violent way, we must also

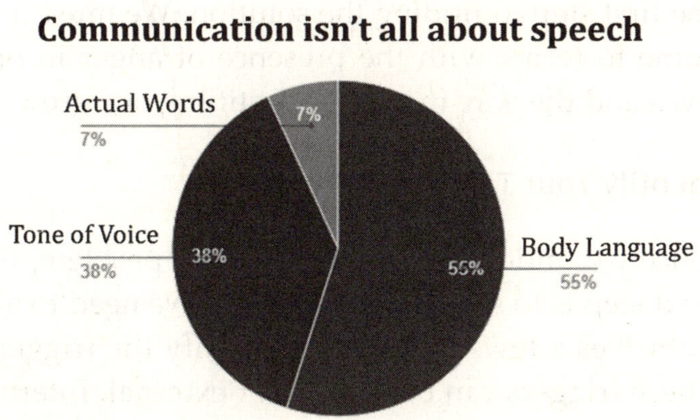

take these more subtle aspects of the process into account. By fine-tuning not just our words but our minds and hearts as well, we can deal with others in more peaceful ways.

4.7. PRACTICE MAKES PERFECT

Most of the time, anger comes out impulsively. If we can somehow stop the eruption and channel it in a positive way, we can gain positive results. Most of us, however, lack the ability to tame our emotions when they arise. But that doesn't mean the art is impossible. Below is a step-by-step process that will help us curb intense emotions when they arise.

Recognize the Problem

Recognizing that we have an anger problem is the first step to finding the solution. We must first come to terms with the presence of anger in our lives and the way in which it's stifling our growth.

Identify Your Triggers

Once we understand that we have a problem, the next step is to search for its causes. We need to ask ourselves a few questions to identify the triggers. These triggers can be internal or external. Internal triggers can be envy, jealousy, competitiveness, ego, etc. External triggers include family members, colleagues at work or other people. If we start analysing these factors, we will be able to see why we are becoming angry. If we have a hard time identifying these stimuli, we can seek help of a friend, counsellor or mentor.

Apply the Solution

Healing the weak spots of our psyche can take a long time. Our mind and body are the internal resting places of anger. To heal these compromised areas, the Bhagavad Gita recommends clarity. Let us now take a look at how we can maintain clarity in our body and mind.

Clarity of Body

1. Prayers

   Once we realize that we are tiny and our problem is huge, we naturally feel the urge to take the shelter of a higher power. Consistent, sincere prayer helps to release some of the mental pressure that the problem creates and thus allows us to maintain a clearer state of being.

2. Respect

   We should respect everyone we deal with, especially those we regularly interact with; family members, colleagues, classmates, etc. You might notice that we usually don't get angry with those whom we deeply respect. By maintaining a respectful mood in which we remind ourselves of all the good qualities a person has, we protect ourselves from outbursts to a great degree. Respect can be contagious; when others notice the respect we extend to them, they'll naturally be inclined to treat us similarly.

3. Cleanliness

   Cleanliness is both internal and external. We keep our body externally clean by bathing at least once a day, preferably twice. We maintain internal cleanliness by not indulging in promiscuity. Illicit affairs and extramarital relationships pollute the heart. They also produce a lot of bad karma. If one remains strictly committed to their significant other, one can maintain a high standard of internal cleanliness.

4. Simplicity and non-violence

   Simplicity means not being duplicitous. Our motto should be 'simple living, high thinking'. We don't need to impress others or try and prove to them that we're happy. It is better to cultivate a simple heart based on high values than to showcase one's material enjoyment. By adapting to a plant-based diet, we remain non-violent to animals. By not hurting others, we remain non-violent to humans.

Clarity of Mind

1. Satisfaction

   Regulating the senses instead of letting them run wild yields satisfaction of the mind. In today's world, we are constantly being allured by various types of sensory enjoyment. In this state of 'What's next?', we can never find satisfaction with what we already have. Try not giving in to the senses' unlimited demands for more and more pleasure. These days social media puts us in competitive mode when we see our friends' achievements, causing dissatisfaction. Instead, compete with yourself. How have you improved from your past self? This comparison will help you trace your weaknesses and strengths. Rather than finding happiness in achievements, find happiness in *working for* the achievements. This will keep us satisfied. Otherwise, we remain happy at the moment of achievement but the next moment our race for another achievement starts. This is unending. That is why our goals should be very internally fulfilling and spiritually uplifting.

2. Gravity

   The best way to train the mind is to monitor and regulate one's thoughts. Spiritual thoughts nourish the mind while frivolous, materialistic thoughts disturb the mind. Through a conscious effort to cultivate spiritual thoughts, we can naturally develop a clearer mentality that is more conducive to patience and peace.

3. Purification

   One of the most powerful ways to combat bad qualities like anger is to actively cultivate good qualities. As previously mentioned, yoga and meditation are useful ways of cleansing the heart of its impurities. While success is guaranteed, the process is a gradual one. With steady spiritual practice, one cultivates good qualities and gives up undesirable ones.

4.8. OUR BEHAVIOUR DURING PRACTICE

Humility

To cultivate humility, we need to develop faith in the fact that we are not this body and our presence in this body is very temporary. We also need to understand that this world is designed in such a way that it frustrates everyone at one time or the other. By being humble, we can easily face any type of situation in this world.

Humility is a divine quality. A person who is humble can serve anyone and deal with anyone. Lord Chaitanya, a divine avatar who appeared in the sixteenth century, said, 'One should be humbler than a blade of grass and more tolerant than a tree. One should give respect to all while expecting none in return.' By imbibing this mentality, we can receive unlimited blessings with which we can develop all the good qualities we desire.

Humility works like a wall that stops us from offending others with our words and actions. If we offend someone due to a lack of control over our senses, we should repent and ask forgiveness. That way, we can maintain a higher consciousness at all times.

Reflective Listening

Reflective listening is a way of communicating in which the listener tries to deeply understand what the speaker is trying to say and then reflect it back to them. In a disagreement, this practice shifts the listener's focus from thinking of how to refute an argument to how to better understand the other person. Even if we disagree with someone, we don't need to throw negativity at them. Once we properly understand the other person's thoughts and feelings, we can respond in a calm and clear way.

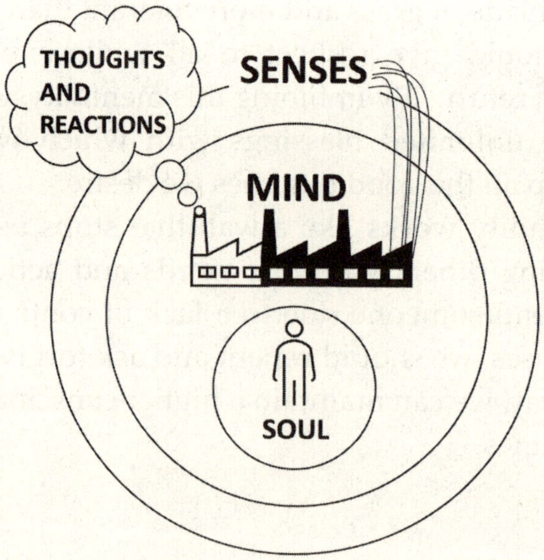

Identify Anger, Don't Identify *with* It

Anger originates in the mind. Let us first understand our internal structure before we go further into this topic. As stated earlier, we are eternal spirit souls living in temporary, material bodies and minds. The mind is a kind of factory that produces all kinds of thoughts and reactions according to what our senses perceive. These thoughts and reactions typically fall under one of the two categories: accepting things we like or rejecting things we dislike. However, what we like and what is actually good for us are seldom the same. Similarly, many of the things our mind rejects are actually beneficial in the long run. We must learn to identify the mind's mood swings instead of identifying *with* them. By understanding one's position as separate from the mind, and by further solidifying that conviction through meditation and yoga and by reading spiritual wisdom texts, one gradually becomes steeped in this liberating understanding. Consequently, whenever the mind presents us with self-destructive emotions like anger, envy, selfishness, etc., we can draw on our power to identify them as useless intruders and ignore their influence.

4.9. CHOOSE YOUR BATTLES

How do we address a situation in which someone is deliberately causing us trouble? How can we solve the problem without getting implicated physically or emotionally? The fact is that such altercations are bound to happen—all we can do is make the conscious choice to limit them as far as possible. What is the way to do this? As the American saying goes, 'Good fences make good neighbours.' Be sure to maintain boundaries between yourself and those around you. There is no need to go poking your nose into others' business unnecessarily and there is no need to allow anyone else to come poking their nose into yours. We always retain the power to choose who we interact with and for what purpose.

We may consider the eagle in this connection. Eagles are some of the highest-flying birds on Earth. Interestingly, sometimes a crow will mount an eagle's back and start pecking at its neck. Surely the eagle suffers in this situation, but it does not try to bite the crow back; it simply flies higher and higher, making it progressively more difficult for the crow to breathe. Finally, the crow gives up and leaves the eagle alone. Similarly, we are bound to come across people who want to pick an argument with us, but instead of indulging them, we should stay firm in character; they will eventually disappear. The nature of crows is to peck necks and eat garbage; don't let them bring you down to their level.

4.10. PATIENCE

The repercussions of an angry outburst can torment the aggressor for years. It is easy to react to provocative situations, but the true measure of a man's character lies in his ability to tolerate them. Through the practice of tolerance, abundant lessons may be learnt and abundant tears may be avoided.

Long ago, there lived a humble family. They were gentle and honest people, but they were also very poor. Eventually, the wife gave birth to a baby boy. As the baby grew, so did the financial pressure on the parents. Finally, the husband told the wife that he was going to go abroad to make lots of money; he couldn't stand to think of his family living in poverty. He did not want his child to suffer. He then struggled for a long time in a foreign country, attempting to find success; having made a promise, he kept trying. After some years, he finally made it big and thus began his return journey. Given the amount of time that had passed, he was worried about how his wife would receive him, so he decided to stay in a hostel across the street from his old home and assess the situation.

Just after sunset, he saw his wife walking home with a handsome young man. Enraged, he began seething with anger; he had worked so hard for her and his son's sake and this is how he was repaid?! He began aching with a need for revenge. Then, a quote he had heard some years prior popped up in his mind: 'One moment of patience can save one from a million moments of regret.' This wisdom brought him back to his senses and he decided to inquire further before making any rash decisions.

He composed himself, reached home and knocked on the door. His wife opened the door and burst into blissful tears. She then brought the young man he had seen earlier and introduced him as his son. When the man had left his home, his son had only been a couple of years old; now he was fully grown. In his mind's angry fog, the man had not considered the effects of the passage of time. Luckily, the power of patience prevailed and saved him from what could have been a bitter tragedy.

4.11. HOW TO CURB ANGER

We can use the F.I.S.H.P.A.R.K. formula to keep our anger under control.

F–Forgiveness

> *It is wise to direct your anger towards problems—not people.*
>
> —William Arthur Ward

Corrie ten Boom was a Dutch watchmaker from Holland. During World War II, when Holland was invaded by Germany, she provided safe shelter to countless Jews who would have otherwise been sent off to concentration camps. Once Nazi officers came to know of this, they arrested her entire family and sent them all to Ravensbrück, the most brutal of all the camps. During their confinement, she lost both her father and sister. After the war, she returned to her hometown and began her watchmaking work again. One day, while at church, she happened to bump into the very guards who had tormented her and her family in Ravensbrück. Despite their cruelty, she forgave them. She later said, 'Forgiveness is an act of will, and it can function regardless of the temperature of the heart. It is a key that unlocks the door of resentment and the handcuffs of hatred.'

Forgiveness is an invaluable virtue. There are inadequacies and mistreatments in every relationship. Without forgiveness, practically all relationships are doomed to perdition. If we refocus our resentment onto the problems making people act a certain way instead of focusing it on the people themselves, forgiveness becomes natural.

I–Identify the Problem

The first step in solving a problem is to identify it. Though many say anger is a natural and healthy emotion, on a case-by-case basis, we must identify whether it is actually productive or not. Uncontrolled anger is a serious problem; controlled anger can be a positive force. We should thus earnestly consider the nature of our anger and determine its actual value.

It is worthwhile to sit and honestly assess our outbursts of anger instead of justifying our anger all the time. It is also helpful to consider the opinions of friends and family members. The questions below will help us understand the nature of our anger.

1. How often do we become angry?
2. What is the nature of our anger?
3. How long does anger and bad mood stay with us?
4. Do we see anger as a reason for relationship problems?

5. Do we have good, lasting relationships with friends and family?
6. Do we see a relationship between our ill health and anger?

S–Speak Less, Listen More

Think before you act; think twice before you speak.

—Thomas Browne

If we cultivate the habit of speaking less and listening more, we not only check the force of anger but also gain valuable time to consider the best things to say. Sometimes, we speak out without considering how our words will affect others. Anger tends to come out like an unstoppable force in the form of harsh words. We should thus recognize the power of words to not only build relationships but to break them as well. By checking the force of our words, we check the force of our anger. Try employing reflective listening instead of bursting out with impulsive speech.

H–Humour

As previously mentioned, humour is a great way to subdue anger. The right joke can completely change the texture of a tense situation. I remember once sitting at an airport gate for an extra two hours while waiting for a delayed flight to begin its boarding process. All of my fellow passengers were clearly disturbed by the delay. Finally, a flight attendant came out and made the announcement that they would start boarding in ten minutes. 'I can guarantee you'll be in the air in thirty minutes. The rest is up to higher authorities,' she said, raising her hands to the sky, indicating that God was in charge. Everyone laughed and thus the tension was somewhat broken. While anger makes the heart heavy, humour makes it light. Never underestimate the power of humour to alleviate a tense situation.

P–Positive Solutions

> *Whenever you are angry, be assured, that it is not only a present evil, but that you have increased a habit, and added fuel to a fire.*
>
> —Epictetus

When something or someone is making us angry, we must analyse the problem and find a solution. Rather than succumbing to the negativity of the situation, we can choose to avoid it altogether. We have full volition to avoid unnecessarily speaking to those who annoy us. We also can learn not to expect much from those persons or things that let us down. By tapering our expectations, we become less prone to incitement upon their not being met. While we may not be able to change others, we can change the way we view and interact with them.

A–Appreciation

How do we change the way we view others? We need to learn to see the good in others. When we start doing that, we tend to admire their good qualities. This will naturally lead to the appreciation of others we interact with. Appreciation makes anyone and everyone happy. It increases the positivity in the environment and improves relationships. If we cultivate this one quality, it will eventually overpower our other weaknesses and improve our quality of life. Appreciation is an act of giving. It deepens and widens the heart. An anecdote comes to mind in this connection. The organizer of a week-long training course told all the course participants to meet and express to each other appreciation and gratitude for being present at and actively participating in the course. Initially, the organizer allocated only thirty minutes for this. As the participants started admiring and appreciating each other, the whole hall filled up with positivity in a few minutes. Everyone started smiling and experiencing the immense joy of giving and accepting appreciation. This lasted more than an hour. You can try this exercise at home or in the workplace. You will experience amazing results.

When we appreciate a person, we subtly position them higher than us. This awakens the quality of humility in us. Humility is a very noble virtue. Recognition of the temporality of our existence in this body naturally makes us more humble. Realization of the fact that everything can be taken away from us at any moment deepens that humility. As we gradually become humbler, we become easier to deal with. Our lack of a sense of entitlement manifests in our ability to tolerate provocative situations. As a result, we naturally become less afflicted by anger and more inclined to live peacefully.

R–Relaxation

Exhaustion and anxiety trigger anger; relaxation subdues it. These days, people generally have very little time to relax. But, just as one must sharpen an axe before cutting a tree, once must replenish the depleted mind before putting it to work. While exhaustion can make one prone to anger over the smallest things, proper relaxation can keep one calm even in the face of the biggest annoyances. The next time you get angry over something small, ask yourself, 'Did I sleep well? Did I eat properly?' When the body is properly cared for, the mind naturally becomes more peaceful. Besides proper rest and a proper diet, yoga and pranayama also help keep the body and mind calm. Aroma therapy, mindfulness and a special technique called Progressive Muscle Relaxation can also work wonders for the restless body and mind. Figure out which one suits you best and make it a habit.

K-Knowledge

The nature of this world is such that we usually don't get what we want. Even if, after spending many years longing for something, we *do* get it, we are often unable to enjoy it for long due to various reasons. One of the most prominent reasons is boredom—how many times have you wound up bored with something you once strongly desired? And yet, without fail, we then start searching for something new, something we're sure will cure us of boredom once and for all. Another spoiler: when we get something we want, it usually comes along with something we don't want. Thus, we lose our taste for the thing we initially desired.

As we suffer through the above process year after year, we eventually become old and leave the world, never having actually satisfied our craving for something eternally satisfying. We know all these things. We hear about them all the time. We watch ourselves and others endure the same process. But, due to our illusions, we neglect this essential lesson of life. What makes the difference is knowledge—we must recognize the brevity of our stay in this world. Such an understanding then motivates us to try and grow flowers of love instead of adding fuel to the fire of our dissatisfaction, and in turn, our anger. Even when we do lose our temper, if we understand the shortness of life and seek forgiveness, we douse the fire of enmity and misunderstanding and thus always remain peaceful.

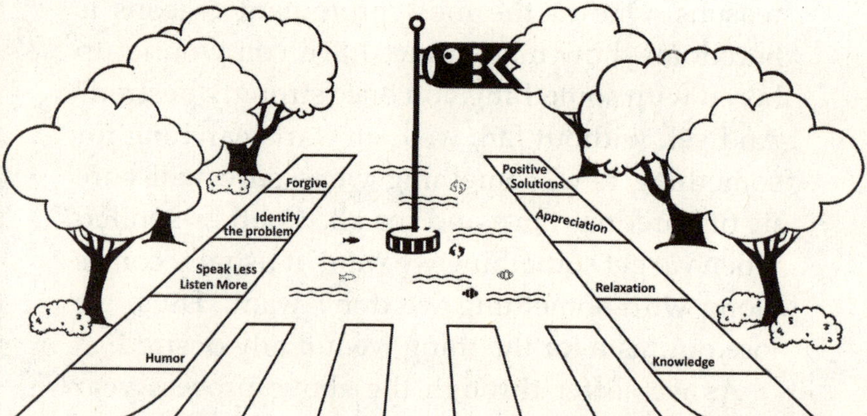

'Conflict Is Inevitable, Combat Is Optional'[10]

Conflict arises due to mismatched expectations. During conflict, both the parties involved share negativity, anger and frustration. Each cannot tolerate the presence of the other. In this situation, water must be used to douse the fire in the form of positivity.

When the mind is racing to convert the conflict into a battle that must be won, intelligence should focus on the negative aspects of 'war' and the losses that may be incurred. Instead of becoming angry and cultivating negative emotions towards the other party, we should use our intelligence to slow down and consider coming to an agreement. When a conflict is inevitable, we have a few choices. We don't need to turn every conflict into a battle. We can look for a win–win solution. For this to happen, one should be determined to end the conflict in a way that benefits both parties. Anger does not let us think of the negative repercussions of combat. For this reason, we should put anger in the backseat. If both parties understand that anger will cause losses, they can come to a consensus on how to end the conflict. If conflict leads to combat, both parties will suffer anyway.

10 A quote by Max Lucado.

A father of two sons passed away, leaving the sons with a huge property to manage. Over the years, the sons developed differences based on trivial matters. Their relationship was almost ruined. They both approached attorneys to claim their share of their father's property. The vast tract of land they surveyed would fetch them a lot of money. However, if they split up the land into two plots and sold it, they would not get nearly as much individually. One of their common friends suggested they bury the hatchet and unite in order to fully benefit from their father's estate. When the brothers understood the stakes, they resolved their differences.

Conflict between spouses is common. Sometimes it goes very far. However, if they happen to be parents and they pause to think about the future of their children, they will patch up their differences and come together for the greater good.

When we enter into conflict with someone, we should make sure we speak carefully so as not to hurt them. We should be careful in how we communicate. We should not belittle but respect them, keeping in mind that they are also a part and parcel of the divine. Rendering a small service to them or speaking words of appreciation or glorification can have a large positive impact.

RELAXATION TECHNIQUES

Progressive Muscle Relaxation (PMR)

Anger tenses our muscles. If we relax our muscles, our mind follows suit. PMR is most effectively performed under the guidance of a teacher, but there are many great videos online that can walk you through it. You will be instructed to tense the muscles in your neck as you breathe in for five to ten seconds and then relax them completely as you fully exhale. As you tense your muscles, picture your life force flowing into the muscles to strengthen them. As you relax, let all of your anger exit your body. By practising this technique on a daily basis, we can become less susceptible to anger.

Different Types of Pranayama

Whenever you feel anxious, drop everything and start doing pranayama for an immediate sense of calm. There are fifteen different types of pranayama, categorized based on three actions: puraka (inhalation), kumbhaka (retention) and rechaka (exhalation). Puraka involves filling the lungs with air. Kumbhaka involves retaining the air for a few moments. Rechaka involves slowly releasing the air and leaving the lungs empty for a few moments before starting over with puraka. While doing this, we must meditate on the flow of air, in and out.

Different Types of Meditation

The mind is the seat of all anger. It can either be our best friend or our worst enemy. While the mind to a large extent remains a mystery to modern science, the ancient wisdom texts offer volumes of literature describing not just the mind but also how to control it. The main process recommended for controlling the mind is meditation, which has now become a buzzword due to its ability to keep one calm and focused. Some practise it for psychological benefits, others for spiritual benefits and still others, for overall wellness. But the key aspect of meditation, regardless of one's aim, is to bring the mind to focus on a single point, to bring the mind back to that point no matter where it wanders. Let's take a look at a few different kinds of meditation. Which one suits you best?

Zen Meditation

Zen is a Buddhist meditation technique. Once comfortably seated with your back erect, focus on your breath. As your breathing normalizes, simply observe it. When distractions arise, you must simply bring your mind back to your breath until your mind becomes still.

Mindfulness Meditation

A healthy mind is fully conscious of its surroundings, thoughts and feelings without being overly reactive. Mindfulness meditation is a process by which one gains complete awareness of the present moment. It is similar to zen meditation in that sense—after streamlining one's breath through uniform inhalations and exhalations, one becomes conscious of it, and when distractions arise, one re-routes the mind to the breath.

Transcendental Meditation (TM)

Even though it uses a mantra, TM is a silent meditation technique in which one focuses the mind on the syllables of the mantra within one's mind. Once one receives the mantra from a TM teacher, one sits and focuses on it for fifteen to twenty minutes daily.

Vipassana Meditation

Vipassana is another Buddhist meditation practice. The practitioner is meant to observe the flow of thoughts coming into and going out of the mind. The idea is to be an objective witness to the thoughts, while not reacting to any of them in a negative or positive way. One also controls one's breathing in a way that helps the mind objectively witness its own activities.

Kundalini Yoga Meditation

Our body has seven chakras or discs of energy, connected to different nerves along the spine. Kundalini is meant to awaken the energy dormant in the root chakra at the base of the spine and spread it to revitalize and replenish the body and mind. The practitioner chants a mantra and practises a specific breathing process. This is perhaps the most complicated of all the practices mentioned and so an expert guide is recommended.

Loving Kindness Meditation

Practitioners of loving kindness meditation generate feelings of love, affection, kindness and compassion for themselves and others. These feelings can be targeted at anyone. It is especially recommended that one directs them towards those one has relational problems with.

Dhyana Yoga Meditation

This is also called ashtanga yoga meditation or the eight-step meditation process. The eight steps are: yama (moral obligations), niyama (moral restraints), asana (yoga postures), pranayama (breath control), pratyahara (withdrawal of senses), dharana (focus), dhyana (meditation) and samadhi (complete absorption). After bringing the body to a balance by following the above initial steps, one meditates on the aspect of God within the heart.

Sonic (Mantra) Meditation

Unlike other organs of our body, the mind is very subtle. We can perceive it through the thoughts it generates. Hence, we need a tool/process that can reach into the mind and rectify its functioning. Mantra meditation stands above other tools in this regard, in that it gives the mind an explicit, positive, spiritual sound to dwell on. As mentioned previously, mantra vibrations deliver us from the agitations of our mind. A mantra, then, is a kind of sonic therapy that delivers the mind from all lower encumbrances.

To understand how mantra meditation works scientifically, we need to understand different brain waves.

THE EFFECTS OF MEDITATION ON BRAINWAVES

Beta waves	When the brain is active and engaged, it generates beta waves. When you are presenting your points in an interview or at a seminar or when you are debugging a software program to solve a production problem, beta waves are at work. They vibrate at a frequency of 16–40 cycles a second.
Sensory motor rhythm (SMR)	Bodily movements like lifting a cell phone to talk to someone or pulling up a chair to sit in are based on the functioning of SMR brainwaves. SMR waves vibrate at a frequency of 12–16 cycles a second.
Alpha waves	Alpha waves are generated when we relax. Work that is not very challenging or simple activities like walking through the woods or watering the plants are examples of engagements that generate alpha waves. The generation of alpha waves makes one relaxed and joyful. Alpha waves vibrate at a frequency of 8–12 cycles per second.

Theta waves	When you automate any activity such that it ceases to involve the active usage of the mind, the performance of that activity produces theta waves. Brushing, taking a bath and driving to office on the same route every day are examples of activities that generate theta waves. We become so familiar with the activity that it runs on autopilot. This is a positive mental state. Theta waves are also generated when we enter the dreaming state before deep sleep. They vibrate at a frequency of 4–8 cycles per second.
Delta waves	Delta waves are activated in deep sleep that is undisturbed by dreams. Delta waves vibrate at a frequency of 1–4 cycles per second. When we want to sleep, switch off the lights, get in bed and close our eyes, our brain slowly switches from highly active beta waves to alpha waves, then to theta waves and finally to delta waves, causing us to enter deep sleep.

When a practitioner sits in a comfortable posture, closes their eyes, starts focusing on the sound vibration and goes deeper and deeper into conscious mantra meditation, their brain slowly shifts to generate alpha waves and our body attains a state of relaxation. As this active meditation process continues, the brain produces more and more alpha waves, leading to an increasing sense of peace and relaxation. It is important to note that, throughout this process, the practitioner is fully active and conscious. In this conscious state, it is possible to infuse the mind with positive qualities like determination, patience, forgiveness, tolerance and the ability to withstand and overcome adversity without losing enthusiasm. This improves our ability to deal with the mind. For this reason, mantra meditation also helps reduce stress and anxiety.

Benefits of Mantra Meditation

In *The Yoga Tradition*, George Feuerstein defines the mantra as follows: 'A mantra is sacred utterance, numinous sound, or sound that is charged with psychospiritual power. A mantra is a sound that empowers the mind.' According to the Sanskrit scholar, Thomas Ashley-Farrand, 'Mantras are energy-based sounds that create thought energy waves.'

A study on Hare Krishna mantra meditation suggests that mantra meditation plays a vital role in the formation of a healthy lifestyle and it helps in the prevention of chronic diseases.[11] Twenty years ago, a study published in the British Medical Journal compared the effects of reciting either the mantra 'Om mani padme ham' or the Ave Maria (Hail Mary in Latin) on respiratory and cardiovascular rhythms.[12] Reciting either of these slowed respiration to six breaths per minute. Electrocardiogram, blood pressure and brain circulation measurements of the people chanting the mantra and reciting the Ave Maria looked the same. These outputs were very different from those associated with spontaneous breathing. The authors concluded that mantras may have beneficial effects on cardiovascular rhythms simply because they slow down breathing.

---

11 https://pubmed.ncbi.nlm.nih.gov/31043916

12 Bernardi, L., Sleight, P., Bandinelli, G., Cencetti, S., Fattorini, L., Wdowczyc-Szulc, J., Lagi, A. (2001). Effect of rosary prayer and yoga mantras on autonomic cardiovascular rhythms: comparative study. *BMJ*, 323(7327), 1446–49.

Another study undertaken at Duke University found that four weeks of practising mantra meditation on a daily basis resulted in significantly decreased levels of stress and anxiety.[13] One study focused on the levels of mental tranquillity achieved while chanting the Hare Krishna maha-mantra ('Hare Krishna Hare Krishna Krishna Krishna Hare Hare/ Hare Rama Hare Rama Rama Rama Hare Hare') on the one hand, and on the other, a made-up mantra composed of meaningless Sanskrit syllables. Those who chanted the maha-mantra were found to have drastically lower levels of stress and anxiety than those who chanted the placebo mantra.[14] The mantra has also been

---

13 Lane, J. D., Seskevich, J. E., & Pieper, C. F. (2007). Brief meditation training can improve perceived stress and negative mood. *Alternative Therapies in Health and Medicine*, 13(1), 38–44.

14 Wolf, D. B., & Abell, N. (2003). Examining the effects of meditation techniques on psychosocial functioning. Research on Social Work Practice, 13(1), 27–42.[6]. Wolf, D. B. (1999). A psychometric analysis of the three gunas. *Pyschological Reports*, 84, 1379–90.

scientifically proven to relieve PTSD in veterans[15] and has even been found to get rid of joint pain![16]

Another study found that kirtan kriya (rhythmic chanting of mantras accompanied by musical instruments) affected gene expression. The practice of kirtan kriya by family members/ caregivers of dementia patients was found to result in the decreased activity of factors that control proinflammatory gene expression and increased activity of factors that control gene expression related to antiviral function,[17] suggesting that this

15 Bormann, J. E., Thorp, S. R., Wetherell, J. L., Golshan, S., & Jang, A. (2013). Meditation-based mantram intervention for veterans with posttraumatic stress disorder: A randomized trial. *Psychological Trauma*, 213(5), 259–67.

16 Monk-Turner, E. (2003). 'The benefits of meditation: experimental findings. *The Social Science Journal*, 40, pp. 465–70.

17 Black, D. S., Cole, S. W., Irwin, M. R., Breen, E., St Cyr, N. M., Nazarian, N., … Lavresky, H. (2013). Yogic meditation reverses NF-KB and IRF-related transcriptome dynamics in leukocytes of family dementia caregivers in a randomized controlled trial. *Psychoneuroendocrinology*, 38(3), 348–55.

mantra-based meditation helps achieve healthier immune function. To assess its effects on cognitive function in individuals with subjective cognitive decline, kirtan kriya was compared to a standard memory-enhancement training programme. Significant improvement in memory was seen with both interventions, but only kirtan kriya resulted in significant improvement in executive function (mental processes that control behaviour).[18] Therefore, mantra-based meditation might be at least as effective as standard treatments for cognitive decline.

MINDFULNESS

Practice Informal Mindfulness

When we do the same things on a regular basis, we tend to enter autopilot mode. In this state, we generally do not put much thought into the things we do. But by being truly mindful of what we do, we can unlock many possibilities that would otherwise pass by unnoticed. To be mindful means

18 Eyre, H. A., Siddarth, P., Acevedo, B., Van, D. K., Paholpak, P., Ercoli, L. Lavretsky, H. (2017). A randomized controlled trial of Kundalini yoga in mild cognitive impairment. International Psychogeriatrics, 29(4), 557–567.

to be fully aware of our thoughts and actions at a given moment. This keeps us in an active and alert state. We can practise this throughout the day by being mindful of each action we perform. This ability to be fully aware is innate to all of us; we need only hone it to realize its presence. Try mindful travelling, mindful eating, mindful talking and mindful listening, and see how your life becomes more lively and serene.

Mindfulness Meditation

Sit comfortably, either on a chair or cross-legged on the ground, and set a timer to five minutes. Make sure your posture is proper. Close your eyes and focus your attention on your breath. Observe how your breath is flowing in and out. It is now that you will start to feel your mind wandering—the email you were supposed to send, the bills you have to pay, the presentation you have to give, etc. Just steadily bring the mind back to your breathing without becoming absorbed in any one thought. Become an objective witness, undisturbed by worry or excitement. Once the timer goes off, observe your mental and physical state, take account of the calmness you now feel that wasn't perceptible five minutes ago. Make a habit of this meditation and work to increase the amount of time you spend meditating for increasingly powerful results.

Mindful Body Scan Meditation

Our physical body is a complex machine with bones, flesh, blood, marrow, etc. Our subtle body is a combination of mind, intelligence and false ego. When there is a problem in the subtle body or the physical body, it becomes difficult for us to function properly. The activities of the subtle body influence the physical body. Hence, we need to take care of both the bodies; mindful body scan meditation does this.

Lie down on a yoga mat or a soft, flat surface or assume any sitting posture you are comfortable in. Focus on each part of your body, starting from your toes and moving up, and observe the sensations you perceive in it—stiffness, pain, tension, whatever they may be—while you take deep breaths. Inhale deeply and pass the breath along to the part of the body you are observing. If there is any tension or discomfort in that part, release it into the ether or bright sunshine as you breathe out. In this manner, scan your whole body.

Do this every day or a few times a day if you have the time. It brings calmness and relief from stress and anxiety.

4.12. MANAGING ANGER IN RELATIONSHIPS

Anger comes forcefully, like a volcanic eruption. If we are not careful, it can melt away even the strongest relationships. Below are some of the damaging effects of unchecked anger on relationships.

1. A perception of distance
2. Diminishing respect
3. Growing distrust
4. Discomfort in the heart of the recipient of the anger
5. Guilt
6. (In the case of children who witness their parents expressing anger) An increasing likelihood of being prone to anger
7. The perception of a lack of personal safety at home

Problems tend to escalate quickly in close relationships. An annoyed look can turn into an annoyed tone, which can escalate into angry words, and finally, a full-fledged argument. While arguments are hard to avoid, we can always control the way we act afterwards. Instead of harbouring a grudge, try doing a good deed for your partner, something that will please them. Even the smallest act of thoughtfulness can completely deflate the situation. If, instead, we let anger dictate how we treat that person, resentment will develop and eventually take root in the hearts of both parties. This ultimately leads to unhappy relationships, and often, divorce. Remember the famous Einstein quote: 'Problems cannot be solved by the same mentality that produced them.' By not allowing anger to dictate our actions outside of angry moments, we can guide our own lives towards interpersonal success.

Below are some of the qualities and habits that we can inculcate to better manage anger-related problems in marriages/relationships.

Respect

The familiarity that develops between people who live with each other tends to lead to fewer apprehensions in them about expressing displeasure. Because all formalities are thrown out of the window, we tend in such relationships to let our thoughts and emotions fly, with scant regard for the impact on the person in front of us.

Instead of becoming overly familiar, try developing a sense of respect for your partner. Our emotions manifest in different ways before those we have a deep respect for. Remember that everyone has a divine presence within them that is worthy of respect; this will soften the edges of your outbursts.

Focusing on People's Good Qualities

Negativity is the root cause of anger. When you start feeling some resentment brewing, try recollecting the good qualities that your spouse possesses instead of becoming absorbed in thinking about the bad ones. This will help subdue negative feelings.

Being Aware of Sensitivities

In a relationship, both parties will always carry with them certain sensitivities that, when prodded, will evoke sudden feelings of intense anger and resentment. We should avoid sensitive subjects as much as possible. When we absolutely must deal with them, we should do so in a very gentle and humble manner.

Maintaining a Strong Balance in One's Emotional Bank Account

Relationships are based on love and trust. When you break the love or trust of your significant other, funds get debited from your emotional bank account. Too many debits in a row will lead to relational bankruptcy. Remember to make deposits in your account by doing affectionate things for your partner or at least saying pleasing words. This will save you from relational poverty.

Appreciation

Appreciation is a cold-water bucket on the fire of anger. It also plays a big role in maintaining the strength of one's emotional bank account. Regularly appreciating one's spouse will ensure a healthy balance. Such appreciation can also be tactically employed in moments when you feel your spouse needs to be corrected. Try sandwiching the correction between two appreciations. This will soften the exchange and make for fewer unnecessary arguments.

Forgiveness

Relationships demand forgiveness. Forgiveness is a cream that helps to heal the cracks in relationships. Rather than getting hung up on who was right and who was wrong, try to forgive and move on. If we fail to forgive, we will never develop the trust necessary for a relationship to be healthy.

Clear Communication

To help prevent anger before it starts, clear communication is key. Misunderstandings arise when we assume things without communicating them properly. Most of the time, we assume that our partner views things and acts in the same way we view things and act. This is where the problem lies. We cannot expect the other person to think the way we do. It is very important to communicate what we are doing and why we're doing it.

I once heard a story about an American man who married an Italian woman. Italians typically covet the last slice of bread because the texture is, to them, more desirable than that of the other slices. The Italian wife, as an act of love, always made sure to save the last slice for her husband. Americans, however, generally detest the end slice. The husband began to feel that his wife was being inconsiderate. This small miscommunication ultimately led to other bigger ones that, in turn, put a serious strain on their relationship. When the issue of the bread surfaced, the man was moved to find that his wife had been caring for him in her own way all along. This clarity helped to ultimately patch up their relationship. The moral of the story—good intentions can easily be soiled by bad communication. Ensure your relationship takes both into account for a smoother road ahead.

United We Stand

When any personality disorders are detected in their children, parents should come together to address them. It is always advisable to take professional help before the problem becomes unmanageable. The behaviour of the child often causes problems between parents, who try to discipline the child based on how they were brought up by *their* parents. The father might think that even though the child is not on the right track, things will become alright, while the mother might disagree and try to discipline the child.

One of the solutions for this type of a problem is for the parents to sit and talk and come to an agreement about who will monitor the child. When children have personality disorders or other mental issues, parents should come together and seek medical help. Otherwise, these issues may cause rifts.

4.13. ANGER AND CHILDREN

If we are cognizant of how our anger can negatively affect our children's health and development, we might take a deep breath and avoid doing serious damage the next time anger arrives like a tornado.

When children regularly see angry outbursts from their parents, they develop fear and insecurity. Their mental growth gets stunted. None of us ever forgets the incidents of our childhood. Some children, in the latter part of their lives, become wild and aggressive, whereas other children develop timidity and unnecessary fear. In extreme cases, some children become sadists and find happiness in hurting and exploiting others.

When children watch their parents regularly quarrel and yell at each other, they often end up thinking that they themselves are the problem. As a result, they develop animosity towards one or both of their parents. When anger is in fact directly targeted towards children in the form of abusive language, they become sad and depressed. If children are physically punished, they become aggressive themselves, which bars them from having healthy relationships with others in the future.

When you see your child doing something wrong, apply self-restraint—don't explode onto the child. Use normal words, not abusive language. If you lose your temper and become angry at your child, ask for forgiveness. This will help your child understand that anger is a part of life, not life itself. Children usually assimilate their personality traits from their parents. Thus, it is best to create a healthy and loving environment in the home that helps foster the positive growth of the child.

If you feel you are often becoming unnecessarily angry and feel unable to curb your anger on your own, it would be best to consult a psychiatrist or a counsellor; otherwise, your children will surely suffer.

SUMMARY

Use the S.A.M.P.L.E. Formula to Release Your Anger in a Safe Way

S–Shift your focus

A–Attain sacred space (reach soul platform)

M–Mantra meditation

P–Pranayama

L–Listen to inspirational lectures

E–Escape the situation

Symptoms of Impending Anger

- Humiliation
- Lack of sleep

- Stress
- Hunger

How to Recover from a Bad Mood

- Remember good times and achievements
- Listen to inspirational lectures
- Learn from your mistakes and move forward
- Remember that it's not the end of the world
- Read spiritual books
- Engage in some constructive activity
- Pray
- Practise yoga
- Practise meditation
- Rest

Apply the T.H.I.N.K. Formula while Choosing Your Words

T–Truthful

H–Helpful

I–Inspirational

N–Necessary

K–Kind

The 7–38–55 Rule of Communication

Our communication is 55 per cent body language, 38 per cent vocal tone and 7 per cent actual words.

Frame Policies and Raise Standards to Avoid Confrontation with Others

Practise Patience as a Cure for Anger

Use the F.I.S.H.P.A.R.K. Formula to Keep Your Anger Under Control

F–Forgiveness

I–Identify the problem

S–Speak less, listen more

H–Humour

P–Positive attitude

A–Apply humility

R–Relaxation (mindfulness, breathing techniques)

K–Knowledge

How to Manage Anger in Relationships

- Show respect
- Remember the other's good qualities

- Beware of sensitivities
- Maintain funds in your emotional bank account
- Show appreciation
- Forgive and move forward
- Communicate clearly

Questions

1. What do you do to maintain and improve the health of your emotional bank account?

____

____

____

____

2. What techniques will you adopt to keep your anger under control?

____

____

____

____

3. How can you improve your communication with others?

____

____

____

____

4. What can you do to recover the next time you're in a bad mood?

____

____

____

____

5. When was the last time you expressed appreciation towards your spouse or a family member?

____

____

____

____

A Note on Sources

All references to religious writings, stories and myths have been taken from the Ramayana, Mahabharata, Bhagavada Gita and Bhagavata Purana, which have been accessed by me in the original Sanskrit. The translation from Sanskrit is my own.

The several quotations in the book have been taken from https://www.goodreads.com/ and https://www.brainyquote.com/.

Yugal Kishore Das

Acknowledgements

I am immensely grateful to my beloved Guru Radhanath Swami, who is the guiding light in my life.

I am grateful to Shyamananda Das from Chowpatty Temple for his support and guidance. I sincerely thank Gauranga Das for his wisdom and inputs on *Anger Management;* Radheshyam Das for his inputs on *Stress Management;* Chaitanya Caran for his suggestions and comments, especially with the book titles.

I sincerely thank Harsha Vardhan Chitta for his encouragement, without which this series would not have come into existence. He has been pushing me to write for the past ten years. He constantly supported this project by providing many much-needed resources. I am grateful to him and his wife Manasa for their warmth and affection.

I am immensely thankful to Prof. Ramana Vinjamuri for his inputs and guidance. He invested his precious time, energy and talent in all the phases of the project. He was involved at every step and in all the important decisions. He drew all the illustrations used in the books and also conceived and designed all the covers. I am deeply grateful to him and his wife Deepti for their continued support in my life. I sincerely thank Dr Shrawan Chittor Surender for his inputs and guidance on this project. I am very grateful to him and his wife Shilpa Surender for their constant support.

I am also grateful to Anupama Das for editing this book. He also many valuable suggestions to make the content appealing.

My sincere thanks goes out to the following: Dr Atul Kapoor, MD (Physician), and Dr Anisha Kapoor, MD (Physician), for their medical advice on *Stress Management*; Dr Kavitha Vasu, MD (Psychiatry), for her time and valuable suggestions on all three books; Dr Alka Desai, MD (Psychiatry), for her inputs on *Anger Management* and *Stress Management*; Dr Padmaja Vuppala, MD (Psychiatry), and her daughter Anusha; Dr Padma Morisetty, MD (Physician), and Dr Uma Pittala, MD (Physician); Dr Dan Fink MD (Physician); Dr Adria Savino, MD (Psychiatry).

I sincerely thank Dr Raman Chopra and his wife Dr Vanita Chopra for their support and encouragement.

I am grateful to my father (late) Satyanarayana Murthy Poolla for his love and affection mother Saraswathi, brother Veerraju, sister Rajyalakshmi for their affection and support throughout my life.

Thanks are also due to Nanda Niketan, Shyam Kishore, Bhagavat Acharya, Sundarhari, Shyamananda Krishna, Ravi Morisetty and Ram Tulasi for their support.

I extend my thanks to HarperCollins for publishing this book. I am grateful to Rakesh Chander and Hina Khajuria and their team, as well as our literary agent Dipti Patel to have made this project a pleasant reality.

And, finally, thanks to all of you readers who accepted the contents of these books with a graceful heart.

About the Author

Yugal Kishore Das is a globally renowned speaker, monk, lifestyle mentor, and coach. He holds a masters degree in mathematics, and bachelors degrees in science and law from various Indian universities. He has also studied software programming.

He is based in Michigan, but has travelled all over the US, imparting spiritual insights on work–life balance, relationships and mindfulness. He has also travelled widely to East Asia, the

Middle East and Europe, conducting seminars on personality development and providing guidance to students, professionals and corporate leaders. He has conducted seminars at universities such as Carnegie Mellon, University of Pittsburgh, University of Cincinnati, Wayne State University and Lawrence Tech University. He has also held seminars for multinational corporations like Procter & Gamble and Ford Motor Company, among others.

His goal is to build like-minded communities and equip them with the tools to address the problems of the modern world and toxic work culture. He believes that people can live in peace and harmony with nature if they have the right tools and support.

Please visit www.yugalkishore.com for more information, and to reach out to the author, please mail at contact@yugalkishore.com.

HarperCollins *Publishers* India

At HarperCollins India, we believe in telling the best stories and finding the widest readership for our books in every format possible. We started publishing in 1992; a great deal has changed since then, but what has remained constant is the passion with which our authors write their books, the love with which readers receive them, and the sheer joy and excitement that we as publishers feel in being a part of the publishing process.

Over the years, we've had the pleasure of publishing some of the finest writing from the subcontinent and around the world, including several award-winning titles and some of the biggest bestsellers in India's publishing history. But nothing has meant more to us than the fact that millions of people have read the books we published, and that somewhere, a book of ours might have made a difference.

As we look to the future, we go back to that one word—a word which has been a driving force for us all these years.

Read.

Harper Collins

4th

HARPER PERENNIAL

HARPER BUSINESS

HARPER BLACK

हार्पर हिन्दी

HarperCollins *Children'sBooks*

HARPER DESIGN

HARPER VANTAGE

Harper Sport